*Flexible Exchange Rates*

EGON SOHMEN

# Flexible Exchange Rates

## Theory and Controversy

THE UNIVERSITY OF CHICAGO PRESS

LIBRARY OF CONGRESS CATALOG NUMBER: 60-14359

THE UNIVERSITY OF CHICAGO PRESS, CHICAGO 37
THE UNIVERSITY OF TORONTO PRESS, TORONTO 5, CANADA

© 1961 BY THE UNIVERSITY OF CHICAGO. PUBLISHED 1961
COMPOSED AND PRINTED BY THE UNIVERSITY OF CHICAGO
PRESS, CHICAGO, ILLINOIS, U.S.A.

*To*

GOTTFRIED VON HABERLER
Mentor and Friend

# *Introduction*

When the decision to create the International Monetary Fund was made at the end of World War II, it appeared as if the money muddle that had worried governments during the interwar period had been resolved. Yet in the thirteen years since the Fund began its operations, balance-of-payments difficulties have plagued its member countries more frequently than ever before. Although recent years have seen a substantial relaxation of exchange controls, they are still possibly more widespread than during the 1930's.

Most people are inclined to disagree with the suggestion that one of the cornerstones of the present system, the pegging of exchange rates, needs to be abolished before a lasting improvement can be expected. The company of ideologies opposing exchange flexibility is a rather mixed one.[1] Some people look upon it as an unashamed expression of Manchester liberalism. On the other hand, the opposition comprises conservatives for whom pegged exchanges seem to offer some of the glitter of the old gold standard.

On closer scrutiny, it is easily seen that these unlikely partners have entirely different conceptions of a system of pegged exchange rates. Conservatives advocate rigidity of exchange rates as part of a general policy of relatively unrestricted free enterprise combined with monetary stability. People with a soft spot for governmental planning, on the other hand, tend to look on conservative credit

---

[1] A few remarks on terminology. We shall use the terms "flexible" and "fluctuating" interchangeably for an exchange rate whose level at any instant is determined in a free exchange market without exchange controls and without prescribed limits of fluctuation (with or without purchases and sales by a stabilization agency). If there is no intervention by a stabilization fund, we shall call the exchange rate "freely fluctuating." Many authors apply the adjective "flexible" to the system of the "adjustable peg" incorporated in the Articles of Agreement of the International Monetary Fund. However widespread this usage may be, it appears to pervert any acceptable meaning of "flexibility."

policies with anything from indifference to amused scorn. Many of them are prone to believe that rapid economic development may, or even must, force governments to sacrifice monetary stability. Disturbingly little attention is paid to the irrefutable fact that the abandonment of the orthodox aims of monetary management is incompatible with a truly pegged exchange rate. As a currency weakens, an exchange rate that had previously guaranteed equilibrium inevitably becomes a disequilibrium rate unless all other countries happen to inflate at the same pace. Official acknowledgment of the depreciation of the currency can be put off temporarily but can never be avoided. Although the painful experience of the postwar era ought to be a sufficiently vivid lesson for all to remember, there still seems to be more than ample reason to point out the damaging consequences of procrastination once the eventual necessity of devaluation is recognized. It is more appropriate to speak of rigged rather than of pegged exchange rates under these circumstances.

Prolonged overvaluation is probably the most undesirable form of exchange-rate "management." More subtle are the disadvantages of the truly *pegged* variety of pegged exchange rates which the conservative wing of the opposition urges upon us. If a system of genuinely pegged exchange rates should be workable without exchange controls, it imposes the **highest** possible standards on monetary and fiscal policies. This in itself is, in my opinion, less deplorable than commonly believed. I would also contend that many economists are far too timid in their appraisal of the workability of monetary policy even in the customary setting. Those governments who—undaunted by the cries of despair of many an economic theorist and the warnings by "realists" that a determined policy of disinflation was politically unfeasible—have boldly experimented with the traditional tools of central banking have seen their efforts amply rewarded. It is high time for a reappraisal of the pessimism the older generation has carried over from the thirties.

But though monetary policy may be better than its reputation, it can be convincingly argued that it is severely handicapped if exchange ratios against other currencies remain rigidly fixed. This simple but centrally important fact is set forth in chapter iv. For anybody who acknowledges the need for smooth and effective countercyclical policy, this alone should prove to be a persuasive argument in favor of exchange-rate flexibility.

In summary, these are the recommendations of this study for the conduct of policy: exchange-rate stability over the long run, achieved not by decree, but rather by alert and flexible monetary policies, and, at least as a long-run objective, without direct intervention in the foreign-exchange markets. It will be argued that whatever government interference seems appropriate in the period immediately following the introduction of flexible rates is best restricted to the forward markets. What many readers would perhaps have found entirely unreasonable only a few years ago, but perhaps not any longer in view of recent experience, is the recommendation of full freedom for all capital movements. As will be shown, the vital function of speculation in a system of flexible exchanges leaves such freedom as the only logical choice.

In spite of these and other slightly unorthodox excursions into the field of economic policy, the larger part of this study is devoted to pure theory. For the sake of a unified treatment, empirical data are nowhere presented, although the author's conclusions on many points would not have been stated with equal conviction in the absence of forceful support by empirical evidence. Such support is available in all the empirical studies undertaken by other authors in recent years.

Among the theoretical arguments that have been used to oppose flexible exchanges the belief that they may be rendered unworkable by low elasticities of import and export demand has long been fashionable. Chapter i shows that it is unfounded.

Chapter ii investigates the effects of capital movements on exchange rates, the volume of credit, the national income, and the terms of trade. A few basic flaws in the traditional analysis of the transfer mechanism are pointed out in the last section.

Many economists lean toward the belief that speculation must accentuate exchange-rate instability when the rates are not pegged. While only practical experience can tell which outcome is more likely in any given situation, the theoretical analysis in chapter iii shows that the presumption that speculation will generally be a stabilizing force is at least equally strong. Apart from a theoretical treatment of forward exchange markets, chapter iv demonstrates that a little help from the monetary authorities can insure that speculation will be stabilizing, although we shall argue that such help will probably be unnecessary after an initial adjustment period during which speculators are taught that they had better dance to the central bank's tune.

A few aspects of income effects of exchange-rate movements are analyzed in chapter v.

Devaluation has almost universally been held to entail inflationary consequences. Many countries with overvalued currencies have opposed exchange-rate flexibility on the grounds that their economies would not be able to withstand the additional inflationary impact of currency depreciation. Chapter vi demonstrates that such fears are unfounded under the conditions in which these countries are likely to find themselves. Policy implications are set forth in the final chapter.

The Appendix presents a brief introduction to the welfare aspects of international trade, essential for an understanding of the basic objectives that underlie many of the policy proposals in the rest of the book.

This monograph developed out of a doctoral thesis submitted at the Massachusetts Institute of Technology in 1958. The preparation of the manuscript was made possible by a grant from the Merrill Foundation for Advancement of Financial Knowledge, to which I extend my sincerest thanks. Charles P. Kindleberger acted as thesis adviser and first sounding board for miscellaneous departures from orthodoxy. I am indebted both to him and to Gottfried Haberler for their patient attention as well as for valuable suggestions. Special thanks are due to Paul A. Samuelson for many stimulating conversations. Discussions with Jaroslav Vanek helped clarify my thoughts in preparing chapters i and v and the Appendix. Sidney S. Alexander, Bela A. Balassa, Arthur I. Bloomfield, Milton Friedman, Hendrik S. Houthakker, and Robert Triffin have read and commented on earlier drafts. I have also benefited from correspondence with Robert E. Baldwin and William H. White. None of them should be blamed for the result, nor should their help be interpreted as an indorsement of any of the policy recommendations advanced in this study. I also had the good fortune of using the editorial services of a classical scholar, Mrs. Margaret Edge. My brother acted as my Dr. Wong.

In the course of writing, I developed a certain sense of urgency for many of the recommended changes which, I hope, is not entirely due to my occupation with the subject during the last three years.

I cannot claim any originality for the basic proposal itself. The wisdom of pegging exchange rates has been questioned by a small but distinguished group of economists.[2] Only a latent suspicion that the majority could not possibly be so far wrong may often have prompted unduly restrained questioning. Whatever shortcomings this book may have, the reader will probably feel that undue restraint is not one of them. Let us hope that these repeated pleas will not pass by entirely unheeded.

[2] F. D. Graham, "The Cause and Cure of 'Dollar Shortage,'" *Essays in International Finance*, No. 10 (Princeton: Princeton University Press, 1949); L. Mints, *Monetary Policy for a Competitive Society* (New York: Macmillan, 1950), chap. v; M. Friedman, "The Case for Flexible Exchange Rates," *Essays in Positive Economics* (Chicago: University of Chicago Press, 1953), pp. 157–201; F. A. Lutz, "The Case for Flexible Exchange Rates," *Banca Nazionale del Lavoro Quarterly Review*, 7, No. 31 (December, 1954), 175–85; G. Haberler, *Currency Convertibility* (Washington: American Enterprise Association, 1954); J. E. Meade, "The Case for Variable Exchange Rates," *Three Banks Review*, September, 1955; W. M. Scammell, *International Monetary Policy* (London: Macmillan, 1957), esp. pp. 86–93, 191–97; also "What Sort of Exchange Rates?" *Westminster Bank Review*, May, 1954; L. A. Hahn, *Geld und Kredit* (Frankfurt: Knapp, 1960), esp. pp. 93–130.

# Contents

# I

# *The Current Account and the Foreign-Exchange Market*

## 1

### BASIC ASSUMPTIONS

This chapter will be restricted to a discussion of the current account in the balance of payments.[1] Since our first objective is a demonstration of the barest fundamentals, a few of the customary simplifications will be adopted. We shall (1) deal with a two-country case and (2) assume that each country produces only a single commodity for export. The latter assumption is made since it does not appear meaningful, or even possible, to associate an elasticity of demand (or of supply) with a group of commodities unless prices and quantities of all members of the group always change in the same proportion. Difficulties would therefore arise for the attempt to establish a rigid link between the market for foreign exchange and the elasticities of the underlying market schedules for commodities and invisibles. These difficulties are of a purely formal kind, however. Supply and demand for foreign exchange are well-behaved functions of the exchange rate even though they may depend on more than one export and one import commodity, and prices and quantities may not be restricted to proportional movements.

[1] Much of this chapter leans on my note "Demand Elasticities and the Foreign-Exchange Market," *Journal of Political Economy*, **65** (1957), 431–36. The figures are reproduced with the kind permission of the *Journal*. The "elasticity approach" to balance-of-payments problems is used in this chapter. Although this approach suffices for the issues raised here, it leaves unanswered many other questions relating to the balance of payments. They will be taken up in later chapters.

(3) Exclusively for the purpose of making possible a simple geometric presentation, infinite supply elasticities, hence constant domestic prices of each country's export commodity, will be assumed. The foreign price of a commodity is then always a scalar multiple of the exchange rate. This assumption is approximately valid in the real world whenever exports are an insignificant proportion of a country's domestic production. Its relaxation merely implies a stretching of the market schedules for foreign exchange, derived by the method described below, without affecting their fundamental properties.

A subject that is usually slurred over too lightly is the exact nature of the commodity demand schedules whose elasticities are supposed to determine the properties of the foreign-exchange market. The usual definition of a "partial" demand curve is that of a locus indicating the quantities demanded of a product when its own price is changed while all other prices are held constant. If aggregate spending on a commodity is an insignificant part of the total volume of transactions and if all cross-elasticities with other goods (whether positive or negative) are small, the partial-equilibrium demand curve is a reasonable first approximation to the *actual* demand curve facing a firm or industry. The latter will have to allow for all possible repercussions in other markets. For the imports of a country as a function of the rate of exchange, the two will in all probability differ beyond recognition. Only a demand curve drawn up under *mutatis mutandis* assumptions can be meaningfully employed for the comparative-static analysis of the exchange market with which we are presently concerned.

At the opposite extreme from a partial demand curve would be a locus of points showing the quantities of a commodity demanded for different (own) prices while *almost* all the rest of the economy (for our purposes, all markets except the foreign-exchange market) is in general equilibrium. The value of the "total" elasticity associated with such a demand schedule would depend, in addition to the partial own-elasticity of demand, on the sign and magnitude of all partial cross-elasticities and any income effects that a price change in this particular market might generate. Even a total demand curve, whatever the institutional arrangements in the economy may be, has to presuppose that the total outstanding volume of credit remains within certain bounds. A "demand elasticity" that allowed for a possibly explosive monetary expansion in response to

[ 2 ]

a given change would be a concept without operational significance. "Total" elasticities in the sense defined above are used everywhere in this book.

<h2 style="text-align:center">2</h2>

## GEOMETRY

The following derivation of the supply-and-demand schedules in the market for foreign exchange from the underlying demand schedules for imports in the domestic economy and abroad is essentially an elaboration of the well-known diagrammatic analyses by F. Machlup[2] and G. Haberler.[3]

Since we assume constant internal prices of each country's exports, the commodity units may be chosen in such a way that these prices equal unity. With this convention, the demand curve for foreign exchange is identical with the demand curve for imports.[4]

The supply schedule of foreign exchange can be derived in the following way: In Figure 1a, demand for exports $X$ is plotted as a function of their (foreign) price, $1/r$. Figure 1b shows the corresponding total revenue curve, $X/r$, again drawn as a function of $1/r$. To obtain total revenue as a function of $r$, we transform it by means of the rectangular hyperbola in Figure 1c which relates $1/r$ to $r$. The transformation is such that the abscissa corresponding to every point, such as $P'$ in Figure 1d equals the value of the abscissa for the corresponding point $P$ in Figure 1b. This yields the required supply function of foreign exchange, $S(r)$.

It is apparent from Figure 1 that the supply schedule of foreign exchange begins to bend backward at the point where the underlying export demand curve has unitary elasticity. This may occur in a region where the demand schedule for foreign exchange is in-

[2] "The Theory of Foreign Exchanges," *Economica*, 1939 and 1940; reprinted in American Economic Association, *Readings in the Theory of International Trade* (Philadelphia: Blakiston, 1950), pp. 104–58.

[3] "The Market of Foreign Exchange and Stability of the Balance of Payments," *Kyklos*, 3 (1949), 193–218.

[4] Given any demand function for imports, $M = f(r)$, the total amount of domestic currency spent on imports is $Mr$, the demand for foreign exchange $Mr/r$, or $D = M = f(r)$ as before. The elasticities of demand for imports and of the demand for foreign exchange will then also be the same.

Throughout this monograph, the rate of exchange $r$ will be defined in the customary (non-British) way as units of domestic currency per unit of foreign currency.

[ 3 ]

elastic enough to give the configuration shown in Figure 2. We notice that the range from $L$ to $U$ is an unstable region, since within its boundaries devaluation will either increase the gap in the balance of autonomous payments (between $A$ and $U$) or reduce a surplus (between $L$ and $A$).

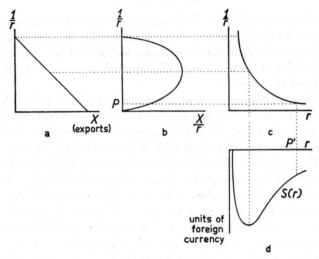

FIG. 1.—Derivation of the supply schedule of foreign exchange, $S(r)$, from the demand function for a country's exports.

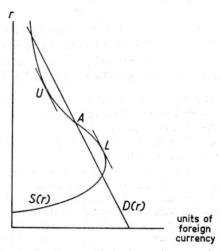

FIG. 2.—Locally unstable foreign-exchange market

[ 4 ]

# 3

The possibility that the foreign-exchange market may be statically unstable has been a favorite topic for discussion among economists for many years. Postulating infinite supply elasticities, the proposition that the sum of the elasticities of demand for imports in two countries must exceed unity if a (small) depreciation of the currency of either country should improve its balance on current account can already be deduced from Appendix J of Marshall's *Money, Credit and Commerce.*[5] As usual, an "improvement" is defined as a reduction of the excess demand for foreign exchange. The theorem is true in this simple form only if (*a*) the elasticities of supply of each country's exports are infinite, (*b*) the balance of trade is initially zero.

Unless the condition is stated in terms of "total" elasticities in the sense defined above, the issue is further complicated by (*c*) the existence of income effects, i.e., changes in the volume of output and employment occasioned by the change in the external balance after a movement of the exchange rate.[6] We choose to work with total elasticities; price and income effects therefore need not be con-

[5] A. Marshall, *Money, Credit and Commerce* (London and New York: Macmillan, 1924). Much of the contents of Appendix J is taken over from Marshall's *Pure Theory of Foreign Trade*, printed for private circulation in 1879.

[6] The principal references for refinements of the criterion, often called the Marshall-Lerner condition, are Joan Robinson, "The Foreign Exchanges," *Essays in the Theory of Employment* (London and New York: Macmillan, 1937), esp. p. 194, n. 1; 2d (1947) ed. reprinted in American Economic Association, *Readings in the Theory of International Trade* (Philadelphia: Blakiston, 1950); A. J. Brown, "Trade Balance and Exchange Stability," *Oxford Economic Papers* Vol. 6 (1942); A. P. Lerner, *The Economics of Control* (New York: Macmillan, 1944), chap. xxviii; A. O. Hirschman, "Devaluation and the Trade Balance," *Review of Economics and Statistics*, Vol. 31 (1949); S. S. Alexander, "Devaluation versus Import Restrictions as an Instrument for Improving Foreign Balance," *International Monetary Fund Staff Papers*, Vol. 1 (1950–51); A. C. Harberger, "Currency Depreciation, Income and the Balance of Trade," *Journal of Political Economy*, Vol. 58 (1950); S. Laursen and L. A. Metzler, "Flexible Exchange Rates and the Theory of Employment," *Review of Economics and Statistics*, Vol. 32 (1950); W. F. Stolper, "The Multiplier, Flexible Exchanges, and International Equilibrium," *Quarterly Journal of Economics*, Vol. 64 (1950). For an excellent summary, see S. S. Alexander, "Effects of a Devaluation: A Simplified Synthesis of Elasticities and Absorption Approaches," *American Economic Review*, 49 (1959), 22–42.

sidered separately. This approach is only meaningful if, as is the case here, the properties of total demand functions relevant for the question being investigated can be unambiguously determined.

"Elasticity pessimism" became a school of thought of considerable weight in the formulation of exchange-rate policy during the years after World War II. Many economists have opposed devaluation of currencies by countries in balance-of-payments difficulties on the grounds that demand elasticities might not be high enough to guarantee that the deficit would be eliminated or reduced. Most authors believed themselves to be compelled to the further conclusion that flexible exchange rates are not feasible under such circumstances.[7]

Whether or not "flexibility pessimism" of this variety is justified is of central importance for the issues discussed in this monograph. The case for flexible exchanges would collapse if a situation were possible in which no statically stable exchange rate existed at all.

[7] A sample of the literature expressing this opinion would include T. Balogh and P. P. Streeten, "The Inappropriateness of Simple 'Elasticity' Concepts in the Analysis of International Trade," *Bulletin of the Oxford University Institute of Statistics*, 13 (1951), esp. p. 66 and the diagrams on p. 76; Brown, "Trade Balance and Exchange Stability," p. 57; P. T. Ellsworth, "Exchange Rates and Exchange Stability," *Review of Economics and Statistics*, 32 (1950), 12; Haberler, "The Market of Foreign Exchange and Stability of the Balance of Payments," p. 194; R. F. Harrod, "Convertibility Problems," *Economia Internazionale*, 8 (1955), 27; S. Laursen and L. A. Metzler, "Flexible Exchange Rates and the Theory of Employment," *Review of Economics and Statistics*, 32 (1950), 282, 295; J. E. Meade, *The Balance of Payments* (London: Oxford University Press, 1951), p. 323; P. A. Samuelson, "Disparity in Postwar Exchange Rates," in *Foreign Economic Policy for the United States*, ed. S. E. Harris (Cambridge: Harvard University Press, 1948), p. 401. A monograph exclusively devoted to this topic is G. Stuvel, *The Exchange Stability Problem* (New York: Augustus M. Kelley, 1951).

H. von Stackelberg concurs with the view that fluctuating exchange rates may be rendered impossible by low demand elasticities in his posthumous essay "Die Theorie des Wechselkurses bei vollständiger Konkurrenz," *Jahrbücher für Nationalökonomie und Statistik*, 161 (1949), 53, although he earlier comes close (pp. 40–41) to realizing the point made below. An English translation has appeared in *International Economic Papers*, No. 1 (London and New York: Macmillan, 1951), page references: 147, 138–39. The only exception to the consensus that low demand elasticities may render free exchange markets unworkable is M. Friedman's *Essays in Positive Economics* (Chicago: University of Chicago Press, 1953), p. 160, n. 4. The theoretical plausibility of static instability in the foreign-exchange market is also questioned by E. V. Morgan in "The Theory of Flexible Exchange Rates," *American Economic Review*, 45 (1955), 279–95.

It is easy to show that this possibility is precluded in the real world. Static instability of the foreign-exchange market due to low import demand elasticities, if it occurs at all, must be a localized exception. Let us assume that the market exhibits an unstable equilibrium such as the one indicated by $A$ in Figure 2. What elasticity pessimists seem to have had in mind is the absence of a stable equilibrium exchange rate *anywhere*. This would require that, as we move away from $A$ in either direction, the two market schedules never intersect again.

Let us first investigate the properties of the schedules as $r$ increases (i.e., as domestic currency depreciates). If the demand schedule were to remain inelastic forever, expenditure on imports in terms of domestic currency would increase infinitely as $r \rightarrow \infty$. With domestic prices assumed constant, the physical quantity of domestic commodities a country is able as well as willing to supply to the rest of the world would eventually have to exceed all bounds. The same follows if supply elasticities are finite as long as domestic prices of exports rise ever so slightly less than in proportion to the depreciation.[8] Since no country has command over infinite resources, the possibility of import demand remaining inelastic is precluded. At worst, unit elasticity must be attained sooner or later. The demand schedule for foreign exchange must eventually become a rectangular hyperbola under the most unfavorable circumstances. For all practical purposes, this extreme possibility can, of course, be excluded. People do not normally persist in purchasing infinitesimally small, but positive, quantities as the relative price of a commodity rises toward infinity. This alone guarantees stable equilibrium at a positive exchange rate after sufficient depreciation, irrespective of the shape of the foreign demand for exports (to be quite exact, exports must not be "super-Giffen goods" for which the quantity demanded declines to zero at a positive price when their price is lowered).

Barring the case of "super-Giffen goods," the supply schedule of

[8] A modified form of "elasticity pessimism" rests on the belief that devaluation may call forth a rise of the domestic price level in exactly the same proportion. Chap. vi will show that there is not even an unambiguous presumption that the price level must rise at all, let alone in proportion to the depreciation, whenever exchange controls and other import restrictions had been in force before the devaluation. Experience has shown that this is almost invariably the case before an "adjustably pegged" currency is devalued. Whether legitimate or unfounded, the fear of inflation is not germane to the issues discussed in this chapter.

foreign exchange can approach the vertical axis only at infinity. Its approach to the axis means that foreign demand for a country's exports becomes perfectly inelastic. Unlike the limiting case of the demand function for imports, however, this type of behavior of the supply function of foreign exchange is entirely realistic. All it requires is that foreign demand for a country's exports should be satiable as their prices approach zero. This has to be expected for most commodities.

These considerations lead us to the conclusion that, even though the relevant elasticities may be very low over a certain range, depreciation in the real world will eventually lead to a stable equilibrium at a finite positive exchange rate.[9] This much has usually been granted by elasticity pessimists, with the qualification, however, that such a rate might be high enough to prove socially and politically unbearable. Although the notion that a more depreciated exchange rate is necessarily less "favorable" on welfare grounds is seriously deficient and does not stand up too well under closer scrutiny, we shall concede it for the time being.

The fatal blow to elasticity pessimism is the existence of another stable equilibrium point *below* the unstable range, i.e., at a more "favorable" exchange rate than any one of the unstable rates. That such a rate exists is easily demonstrated by the same reasoning we used above to deduce the existence of the upper stable equilibrium, bearing in mind that an infinite exchange rate for one currency is equivalent to one of zero for the other.

Any lingering doubts will be immediately dispelled by noting the symmetry between the two countries. Writers on the foreign-exchange market have usually been exclusively concerned with the consequences of low elasticities for the deficit country. The Marshall-Lerner condition, as well as any of its modifications, applies to the surplus country in precisely the same way, however. A small devaluation will not only accentuate the excess demand for foreign exchange by the deficit country if the elasticities are below the critical level; the country with a surplus will find as well that its balance on current account deteriorates when its currency is de-

[9] As a *purely theoretical* matter, the market schedules for foreign exchange may not converge at any finite exchange rate, as can be seen from the considerations above. The nature of this freak possibility will be discussed in greater detail below.

valued.[10] Once it is realized for one country that a stable rate will necessarily be reached eventually if the depreciation is carried far enough, the inherent symmetry of the Marshall-Lerner condition assures us that the same must hold for its trading partner. A stable equilibrium above the region of instability from the point of view of one country is equivalent to one below the unstable range for the other country, and our conclusion necessarily follows.

The point is illustrated even more persuasively by a *reductio ad absurdum*. Let us suppose that no positive stable equilibrium rate existed below the region of instability. The exchange authorities of the deficit country could then decree the exchange rate $r = 0$, equivalent to an infinite appreciation of their currency. In the absence of a lower point of stability, the balance of payments of the former deficit country must now have turned into a surplus. But that country would enjoy another priceless and unprecedented advantage: with finite domestic prices of each country's export commodity, an exchange rate $r = 0$ implies that it would be able to import any desired quantity of foreign goods free of charge. For those who enjoy such meditations, the argument can be pushed beyond absurdity: if no stable equilibrium existed even at an exchange rate of zero, a country could achieve positive trade balances at *negative* rates of exchange. In other words, the rest of the world would be willing as well as able to pay a net *subsidy* on every commodity unit shipped to this country.

Marshall had already pointed out that every unstable range of exchange ratios must be bounded by stable equilibria.[11] It is surprising that this should have been forgotten during the long controversy over the elasticities of import demand, though Marshall's analysis has been reproduced many times, most exhaustively in J. E. Meade's *Geometry of International Trade*.[12]

In a somewhat unusual attack, J. Bhagwati and H. G. Johnson have claimed that the argument outlined here was only accepted as

[10] Strictly speaking, the statement is always true only if the change in the balance of trade is measured in the same currency in both cases. Given an initial imbalance in the current account, devaluation may result in an improvement of the balance when it is measured in one currency, in a deterioration when measured in the other. See Hirschman, "Devaluation and the Trade Balance," pp. 50–53.

[11] A. Marshall, *Money, Credit and Commerce.*

[12] London: Allen & Unwin, 1952.

[9]

valid because "the conclusion purportedly reached is of sufficient propaganda value."[13] The two authors use Marshallian offer curves in an attempt to disprove Marshall's contention concerning the necessity of stable equilibria. It is instructive to review the main point at issue in these terms. The configuration Bhagwati and Johnson present as a realistically possible exception to our conclusion is shown in the positive orthant of Figure 3. Let us assume that the offer curve of country $B$ starts from the origin, as usual, and eventually intersects the horizontal axis, indicating satiation of the residents of country $B$ with the export commodities of $A$. The offer

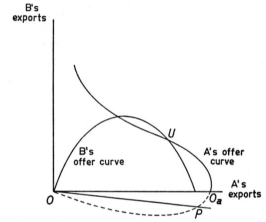

Fig. 3.—Offer curves with unstable equilibrium. One of the stable equilibria bordering the unstable region occurs at non-positive terms of trade.

curve of country $A$, on the other hand, originates not at the origin, but from a point $O_a$ on the horizontal axis beyond the satiation point of country $B$. No stable equilibrium at a finite positive exchange ratio exists to the right of the unstable intersection $U$.

The two authors are silent on whether country $A$'s offer curve is (1) supposed to coincide with the axis from $O$ to $O_a$ or (2) whether the possibility of its extending below the axis (such as the dotted curve in Fig. 3) is admitted. In either case, the offer curve intersects the origin at a non-positive angle.

[13] "Notes on Some Controversies in the Theory of International Trade," *Economic Journal*, **70** (March, 1960), 93, n. 1. The statement refers to my note, "Demand Elasticities and the Foreign-Exchange Market," *Journal of Political Economy*, **65** (1957), 431–36.

The slope of the ray from the origin to any point $P$ on an offer curve equals the domestic price ratio at which a community demands and supplies the quantities of imports and exports indicated by the location of $P$ with respect to the origin $O$. An offer curve whose path through the positive orthant starts at $O_a$ would require that the export commodity of country $A$ be a free good or a "discommodity," in other words, that (1) an amount up to $OO_a$ could be produced at zero or negative marginal cost *and* that (2) its consumption yield zero or negative marginal utility to all residents of $A$. It may also be noted that, as is easily seen from Figure 3, an offer curve originating at a positive distance from the origin is not sufficient for creating an exception to the rule that both stable equilibria bordering the region of instability must be finite. An exception would require that production at zero or negative marginal cost and zero or negative marginal utility of consuming $A$'s exports be not confined to country $A$, but also describe the situation in country $B$ at the point of trading equilibrium.[14]

4

CONSEQUENCES FOR A SYSTEM
OF FLEXIBLE EXCHANGES

A free market will shy away from a point of unstable equilibrium. A freely fluctuating exchange rate can therefore never come to rest at an unstable level. Elasticity pessimism, provided that it ever had any basis at all, can only be justified if the exchange rate is pegged by decree, but it cannot serve as an argument against fluctuating exchange rates.[15] If an economy should ever find itself in the

[14] For further details, see my "Comment" and the "Reply" by Bhagwati and Johnson in a forthcoming issue of the *Economic Journal*.

[15] A necessary condition for the possibility of a stable equilibrium in the foreign-exchange market is that the general-equilibrium system of each of the two economies separately should have a stable solution. While the attempts at a formal existence proof under fairly general conditions are still under way, there is little doubt on the basis of empirical evidence that this is a purely theoretical, not a practical, problem. Cf. K. J. Arrow and G. Debreu, "Existence of an Equilibrium for a Competitive Economy," *Econometrica*, 22 (1954), 265–90.

Most of the literature on foreign exchange deals with the case of two countries. An exception is J. J. Polak and T. C. Liu, "Stability of the Exchange Rate Mechanism in a Multi-Country System," *Econometrica*, 22 (1954), 360–89. We do not endeavor to pursue the issue beyond the two-country case. The formidable

vicinity of an unstable equilibrium point such as $A$ in Figure 2, not only will appreciation of an *administered* exchange rate eventually create a surplus in its balance of autonomous payments, but a freely fluctuating exchange rate may move downward and thus improve the country's terms of trade.[16] More important, the authorities always have the power to push the exchange rate toward its lower rather than its upper stable equilibrium. This can be done by sudden and massive sales of foreign exchange, obtained from the reserves of a stabilization fund or through a short-term loan from abroad, until the supply schedule of foreign exchange is pushed far enough to the right to leave only the lower (stable) equilibrium intersection with the demand curve for foreign exchange.[17] Once the exchange rate remains in the neighborhood of the lower equilibrium point, foreign exchange can be gradually repurchased by the central bank. An attractive feature of such an operation is its profitability for the exchange authorities. They sell foreign exchange when its price is high and repurchase it when it is low.

The possibility of retaliation by the foreign country or countries presents an interesting problem in bilateral monopoly. The exchange authorities abroad would usually have every reason to move the exchange rate to the opposite equilibrium level. A situation of this kind appears unreal enough to warrant the conclusion that a statically unstable equilibrium in the foreign-exchange

---

complications that arise are the same as those we face in the attempt to prove the existence of a stable equilibrium in a competitive economy, the subject of the article by Arrow and Debreu cited above.

[16] Given sufficiently high elasticities of supply (see Joan Robinson, in *Readings in the Theory of International Trade*, p. 400). The controversy over whether depreciation may as a rule be expected to worsen or to improve the terms of trade has filled many pages in the journal literature. Cf. the bibliography given in F. Machlup, "The Terms-of-Trade Effects of Devaluation upon Real Income and the Balance of Trade," *Kyklos*, Vol. 9 (1956); and chap. ii, sec. 4 below. The issue is simplified if the exchange market is unstable, however. As G. Haberler has shown, the exchange rate and the terms of trade always move in the same direction in a region in which the Marshall-Lerner condition is not fulfilled. "Currency Depreciation and the Terms of Trade," in *Wirtschaftliche Entwicklung und soziale Ordnung*, J. Messner and E. Lagler, eds. (Vienna: Herold, 1952), pp. 149–58.

[17] The same result can be achieved by sales of forward exchange. This would eliminate the need to possess (or acquire) foreign exchange reserves first. See chap. iv below.

market is, to put it mildly, a highly unlikely phenomenon. This view is also supported by the empirical observation that black-market exchange rates for currencies of deficit countries have universally been less favorable to these currencies than the official rates. If exchange markets had ever been statically unstable, there would have been an equal chance for the free rate to move to a level favoring the deficit country's currency.

It is often argued that demand elasticities in international trade are substantially higher in the long run than in the short run, owing to the fact that exporters and importers react to movements of the exchange rate only after a certain time lag. Many writers have expressed the fear that high long-run elasticities may not be sufficient to guarantee the practical workability of a flexible exchange system, since low elasticities in the short run might nevertheless render the foreign-exchange markets highly unstable. This view neglects the effects (a) of arbitrage between organized commodity and stock exchanges in different countries and (b) of speculation in foreign exchange. If long-run elasticities are high enough to guarantee a unique stable equilibrium level for the exchange rate, the operations of profit-maximizing arbitrageurs and speculators can be confidently expected to hold the actual market rate at any time close to that level, irrespective of short-run instability.[18] A necessary requirement for speculation to perform its function properly is, of course, freedom of international capital movements.

It is theoretically conceivable that a deficit country's supply and demand schedules of foreign exchange are such that *no* unstable equilibrium exists anywhere while a small devaluation increases the negative balance on current account.[19] It is widely held for this case that devaluation to the stable (and in this case necessarily less "favorable") equilibrium rate of exchange, whose existence follows

[18] Chap. iii will be devoted to an analysis of speculators' behavior.

[19] The implied shape of the market schedules for foreign exchange can be visualized with the aid of Fig. 2. It has been suggested to me that it may have been this constellation which most elasticity pessimists had in mind. The literature does not corroborate this view. Whenever an author used diagrams, he depicted an unstable *equilibrium*. The Marshall-Lerner condition in its crudest form assumes equality of export and import values and hence an unstable equilibrium if the sum of the demand elasticities is less than unity. The notion that flexible exchange rates may not work because demand elasticities might turn out to be too low implied the view that only an unstable equilibrium and no stable ones might exist.

by the reasoning above, whether by decree or through automatic adjustment of a fluctuating rate, necessarily lowers a country's "potential welfare"[20] and that it is therefore in a country's interest to keep the exchange rate pegged at the disequilibrium level. To the extent that this reasoning merely wants to assert that a larger import surplus, *other things being equal*, enables a country temporarily to have command over a larger amount of resources, it is trivially true. The question whether the deficit can be financed at all is frequently neglected, as is the fact that larger current consumption, provided it can be achieved, forces a downward adjustment on the disposable social product in future periods, unless it can be shown that the magnitude of free foreign aid can be made to vary in direct proportion to the deficit in the foreign balance.

In the real world, countries are usually forced to adjust the size of their trade deficits to the available international reserves rather than vice versa. The real choice for the long run, therefore, rarely concerns the *size* of the deficit, but rather the different *ways* in which it can be held down to a certain permissible level. The refusal to use exchange-rate adjustment for this purpose leaves deflationary monetary and fiscal policies or direct controls on imports as the only remaining alternatives. The former may perhaps be effective and relatively painless in more instances than is generally conceded, but they are undoubtedly too painful a remedy in many other cases.

The view that the imposition of direct controls on imports is preferable on welfare grounds to adjustments of price variables became surprisingly popular after World War II. Yet it should not be too difficult to see that the limitation of the deficit on current account to a prescribed level per unit of time through direct controls is a priori unlikely to permit a higher level of potential welfare than the realization of the same value of the foreign balance through price and exchange-rate adjustments. This judgment has to be qualified in one essential respect. Limited trade and exchange controls can increase a country's potential welfare level through exploitation of its monopoly power versus the rest of the world. This is Sidney Alexander's case for direct controls in preference to devaluation.[21] What unsuspecting readers are liable to overlook is (a) that the terms-of-trade argument for controls is an argument for *limited*

[20] See the Appendix for details on the terminology.

[21] Alexander, "Devaluation versus Import Restrictions as an Instrument for Improving Foreign Balance," pp. 379–96.

[ 14 ]

controls and that potential welfare must decline once controls reduce trade below a certain level; (*b*) that Alexander's argument can therefore always be used to favor the introduction of limited controls in an imaginary situation of *entirely unrestricted* trade, but not in the real world where innumerable other trade restrictions are already in effect and nobody knows whether or not they exceed the "optimum" level; (*c*) that no country exports just one single product, but a great many different commodities with different demand elasticities. The imposition of controls across the board, as usually practiced to cope with foreign-exchange difficulties is—to the extent that it is capable of improving potential welfare at all—an extremely crude instrument compared with selective tariffs that take the differences between individual demand elasticities into account.

In conclusion, a few curiosities:

The strength of elasticity pessimism varies considerably with the issue concerned. Many of our British colleagues, for example, have in the years before the recent improvement of the United Kingdom balance of payments repeatedly discounted devaluation of the pound as an effective measure to relieve pressure on sterling. On the other hand, all fears of low elasticities seemed to have been forgotten in the campaign of 1957 to have West Germany appreciate the mark. Sufficient faith in their previous convictions would have compelled them to wonder whether *de*valuation of the German mark might not be a more appropriate step to reduce the German export surplus.

Not infrequently, elasticity pessimists have been strong advocates of trade restrictions for the protection of infant industries. Whenever foreign reciprocal demand is inelastic, however, there is a presumption that the physical volume of imports will *increase* after tariffs are raised.[22] Infant industries might require protective *subsidies to imports*. The reader may note that the issue here is only moderate inelasticity of one country's reciprocal demand, not the simultaneous occurrence in two countries of the much lower elasticity values that could make the foreign-exchange market unstable.

It is sometimes asserted that the relevant demand elasticities are necessarily lower nowadays, given the increase in the number of

[22] See L. A. Metzler, "Tariffs, the Terms of Trade and the Distribution of the National Income," *Journal of Political Economy*, **57** (1949), 1–29.

giant corporations, than they used to be in the more competitive markets of pre-World War I. This argument involves a confusion between the demand curves facing a single firm and a whole industry. While it is conceivable that a perfectly competitive industry reaches its equilibrium in the inelastic range of the industry's demand curve, this can never happen for a monopolist or a monopolistic competitor unless his marginal cost is negative.[23] The more an economy is infested with market imperfections, therefore, the *stronger* is the presumption that the relevant elasticities of demand exceed unity.

It should also be realized that a low demand elasticity for a particular commodity in a given country, or even in the world as a whole, does not imply low demand elasticities for each seller country. The demand for wheat is usually considered to be highly inelastic. What is relevant when Argentina, to give an example, contemplates devaluation, is the demand for *Argentine* wheat, which may be highly elastic.

Many attempts have been made to estimate demand elasticities of internationally traded commodities. Almost without exception, these measurements have yielded elasticities so low that serious doubts seemed to be justified about whether foreign-exchange markets in the countries concerned could be statically stable in the neighborhood of the exchange-rate values in effect at the time of measurement.[24] In view of our theoretical result that static instability must, if it occurs at all, be restricted to a limited range of exchange-rate values, the plausibility of these results is highly questionable. We shall not discuss the reasons why empirical elasticity measurements are likely to be grossly inaccurate. They

[23] Profit maximization requires equality of marginal cost and marginal revenue; hence, marginal revenue will be positive at the equilibrium output of a monopolist as long as marginal cost is positive. Positive marginal revenue, in its turn, implies an elasticity of demand greater than one. This point has been made in H. Brems, "Foreign Exchange Rates and Monopolistic Competition," *Economic Journal*, 63 (1953), 289–94.

[24] The best known studies in this field are T. C. Chang, *Cyclical Movements in the Balance of Payments* (Cambridge: Cambridge University Press, 1951); and J. H. Adler, E. R. Schlesinger, and E. van Westerborg, *The Pattern of United States Import Trade since 1923* (New York: Federal Reserve Bank of New York, May, 1952). A comprehensive bibliography can be found in H. C. Cheng, "Statistical Estimates of Elasticities and Propensities in International Trade," *Int. Mon. Fund Staff Papers*, 7 (April, 1959), 107–58.

have been ably stated by a number of authors.[25] Their arguments are sufficiently convincing to make attempts at correct estimation of the relevant elasticities appear as wasted effort. Observation of the balance-of-payments effects of actual changes of exchange rates in recent years and indirect inference on the elasticity values that must have prevailed seems more promising as well as simpler.

[25] In particular, G. H. Orcutt, "Measurement of Price Elasticities in International Trade," *Review of Economics and Statistics*, 32 (1950), 117–32; F. Machlup, "Elasticity Pessimism in International Trade," *Economia Internazionale*, February, 1950, pp. 118–37; D. J. Morgan and W. J. Cortlett, "The Influence of Price in International Trade: A Study in Method," *Journal of the Royal Statistical Society*, Ser. A, Part III (1951), pp. 307–52.

# II

## *Capital Movements under Flexible Exchanges*

In the preceding chapter, we considered a foreign-exchange market without autonomous capital movements. Supply and demand of foreign exchange were based exclusively on the demand for imports of goods and services in the two countries. The capital account (including official transactions) was supposed to respond passively to imbalances in the current account. This unrealistic restriction will now be relaxed. We will consider only the spot market. Complications arising from the existence of forward markets are taken up in chapter iv.

There are four ways of financing an imbalance in the current account (it will be convenient for our purposes to distinguish primarily according to motive rather than transactor):[1]

a) private gifts and intergovernmental assistance either in the form of loans or of unilateral grants;

b) changes in the official reserves of gold and foreign exchange held by the central bank or a separate stabilization agency ("compensatory official financing," according to the definition of the International Fund in its *Balance of Payments Manual*);

c) gold movements undertaken by private transactors;

d) private capital movements.

The motives for the first group of transactions are outside the realm of economic analysis. Official transactions of the second kind typically respond passively to other factors. The last two types of operations, on the other hand, have customarily been the domain of

---

[1] For a more extensive discussion of the individual items entering into a country's balance of payments, see J. E. Meade, *The Balance of Payments* (London: Oxford University Press, 1951), Part I; and the International Monetary Fund's *Balance of Payments Manual*.

"economic men" and deductions based on the assumption of maximizing behavior are appropriate. They will occupy us in chapters ii to iv. Their analysis will also provide a better understanding of what the guiding principles of compensatory official financing ought to be. It has often been assumed in discussions of exchange-rate flexibility (and has usually been held against the system) that capital transfers are necessarily unpredictable and erratic when exchange rates are not pegged. Neither theoretical considerations nor practical experience lend support to this view. It is one of the central theses of this study that the conscious exploitation of private capital movements is, when exchange rates are flexible, one of the most effective, though neglected, tools of economic policy.

The present chapter is devoted to the *consequences* of movements of gold and capital rather than their motivation. The topic has been extensively treated in the literature.[2]

1

## EFFECTS ON THE FOREIGN-EXCHANGE MARKET

The effects of capital movements on the foreign-exchange market are straightforward. An autonomous inflow of funds, for example, increases the supply of foreign exchange exactly as if exports of goods and services had increased by the same amount.[3] Since the foreign-exchange market must have been statically stable before the disturbance under a regime of fluctuating rates, an inflow must lead to appreciation, an outflow to depreciation, of domestic cur-

[2] The following monographs are available: C. Iversen, *Some Aspects of the Theory of International Capital Movements* (Copenhagen: Munksgaard, 1935); R. Nurkse, *Internationale Kapitalbewegungen* (Vienna: Springer, 1935); C. P. Kindleberger, *International Short-Term Capital Movements* (New York: Columbia University Press, 1937); M. Fanno, *Normal and Abnormal International Capital Transfers* (Minneapolis: University of Minnesota Press, 1939); A. I. Bloomfield, *Capital Imports and the American Balance of Payments* (Chicago: University of Chicago Press, 1950).

[3] The reader will notice that we speak here of movements of "funds" rather than of "capital" since capital movements can cause changes in exchange rates only to the extent that they induce shifts in the market schedules for foreign exchange (currency and bank deposits). The acquisition of foreign bonds against a three months' draft rather than cash, for example, leaves the exchange rate temporarily unaffected (unless the payee covers himself against the exchange risk and swift interest arbitrage instantaneously puts pressure on the spot rate).

rency. The consequences of *gold* shipments on the market for foreign exchange are indistinguishable from those of commercial exports and imports, although they are, of course, prompted by different considerations.

## 2

### MONETARY EFFECTS

Newly imported gold that is deposited with banks can serve as the base of a multiple expansion of credit in a regime of fractional reserve banking. Gold exports have the opposite effect.

The monetary effects of private capital movements depend on the policies adopted by the authorities. If exchange rates are pegged, the monetary consequences of international transactions are precisely the same as they would be under the gold standard. The central bank's commitment to purchase and sell foreign exchange at specified rates of exchange causes changes in bank deposits identical to those prompted by its purchases and sales of gold, for bank reserves are created or extinguished by the same amount.

There are varying degrees of rigidity in a system of pegged exchange rates. The rates at which central banks buy and sell foreign exchange usually differ by a small margin. The margin may be smaller or larger than the average spread that used to exist between the gold points. The mechanism of adjustment to capital movements under genuinely "pegged" exchange rates can be said to be strictly identical to that under the gold standard only if the central bank's margin is roughly the same as the typical spread between the gold points. Capital movements under pegged exchange rates may lead to purchases and sales of foreign exchange by the central bank only when the exchange rate is driven to one of the boundaries of the profit margin. Similarly, capital movements under the old gold standard could lead to gold flows only when the exchange rate was driven to one of the gold points. As long as an exchange rate hovers somewhere between the boundary values at which the central bank begins its pegging operations (or between the gold points), it is effectively a freely fluctuating one. The monetary effects are then those typical of fluctuating rates, i.e., they are absent except for transitory disturbances (see below). The wider the spread between the exchange-rate pegs, the more closely does the system approach fluctuating rates. A widening of exchange-rate

[ 20 ]

pegs alone is, of course, wholly illusory if a currency remains permanently at one of the boundaries of fluctuation as a result of the country's economic policies. The central bank may, furthermore, not confine its intervention on the exchange markets to times when the rate reaches its boundaries. Any purchase and sale of foreign exchange by the central bank causes the monetary effects described above, even though the exchange rate may fluctuate between the officially established pegs.

For expository purposes we shall occasionally assume a hypothetical, "pure" system of pegged rates in which there is no spread at all between the central bank's buying and selling rates for foreign exchange. Such an arrangement exhibits the characteristics of pegged rates most clearly.

Central banks have the power to counteract changes in reserves arising from international transactions by discretionary measures elsewhere. Sterilization of capital movements in a way contrary to the rules of the gold standard is particularly likely if exchange-rate stabilization is undertaken through the intermediary of an independent stabilization fund rather than by the central bank itself.[4] The fund may, for example, finance the acquisition of foreign exchange by issuing debentures of its own. No expansion of the money supply can take place under these circumstances when the stabilization fund purchases foreign exchange.

The right of central banks to exercise discretionary action and thus to "sterilize" movements of gold and capital is now almost universally recognized, in contrast to public attitudes during the gold-standard era. This fact is primarily responsible for the largely erroneous impression that a regime of exchange rates pegged within a narrow margin under a pure paper standard is radically different from the regime of the old gold standard. The renunciation of the outward rituals of the gold standard does not—barring the imposition of exchange controls—automatically enable central banks to exercise the additional discretion they are accorded in principle. From the point of view of a *single* country, and as long as the authorities are determined to preserve the peg without resorting to exchange controls, there is little difference. A country with a paper currency and rigidly pegged exchange rates will have to adjust its

---

[4] For details, see F. Machlup, "The Theory of Foreign Exchanges," *Economica*, N.S., Vol. 6 (1939–40); reprinted in AEA *Readings in the Theory of International Trade* (Philadelphia: Blakiston, 1950), pp. 137–44.

domestic policies to the development of its balance of payments in about the same degree to which it would be compelled to conform by the operation of the old gold standard.[5] It is well known, moreover, that actual movements of gold were never as significant as today's beginning student is led to believe by the textbook version of the gold standard. The brunt of the burden of adjustment was borne by capital movements even during the era when private individuals were entitled to unrestricted international gold transactions at fixed prices. We shall analyze these factors in the two following chapters.

Capital movements have altogether different monetary consequences under a regime of freely fluctuating exchange rates. If the central bank does not intervene in the foreign-exchange market, an autonomous inflow of funds, for example, cannot lead to an increase in the legal reserves of commercial banks (where the banks' deposits with the central bank provide the legal reserves against their own liabilities, as in the United States). If the banking system was fully loaned up, no expansion of credit can take place after an inflow of funds. In the absence of statutory reserve requirements, the acquisition of additional holdings of foreign exchange by private banks after a capital inflow may nevertheless encourage them to expand the volume of deposits. In view of the usual reluctance of bankers, when exchange rates fluctuate freely, to take a position in foreign exchange beyond the minimum balances required for the financing of regular trade, such acquistions will, however, generally remain temporary. It is therefore realistic to assume that every autonomous inflow of funds will be made available to commercial traders.[6] The price of foreign currency must fall sufficiently to in-

[5] For a world of pure paper currencies, there is the obvious difference that all countries together can inflate or deflate in step with each other, whereas world-wide inflation under a universal gold standard is strictly limited by the supply of newly mined gold and the degree to which fractional reserve banking is practiced.

[6] Part of the additional supply of foreign exchange may be temporarily absorbed by speculators. Absorption of an autonomous flow of funds by speculators means complete sterilization. Such funds will merely change ownership between residents of different countries, but will exercise no effect either on the level of the exchange rate, the volume of credit, or the national incomes of the two countries.

It must be expected that the reaction of speculators is as described above if there had been "speculative equilibrium" before the inflow of capital. As outlined in the preceding chapter, a fluctuating exchange rate must necessarily come

duce importers to absorb the additional supply of foreign exchange through increased purchases abroad. This solves the "transfer problem" in the short run.[7] The exchange rate will yield to perform whatever part of the needed adjustment other more sluggish variables such as prices or real incomes are unable to effect.

There is one important qualification. Although it was demonstrated in chapter i that "total" elasticities must be large enough to guarantee stable long-run equilibrium in the neighborhood of an exchange rate actually realized in a free exchange market, it is not to be expected that the reactions of regular commercial exports and imports are swift enough to respond immediately to sudden bursts of capital flows. In the *shortest* run, it can legitimately be assumed that regular export and import demand and supply are relatively inelastic. Several buffers are available, however, which are all but neglected in the literature. One of the most significant ones, at least for the currencies of the large trading nations, ought to be arbitrage between the leading commodity and stock exchanges in the countries concerned. In equilibrium, the quotations on organized exchanges for the same items, compared on the basis of the ruling exchange-rate structure at any moment, must be identical except for brokerage and transport costs. As soon as an exchange rate is disturbed, opportunities for profitable arbitrage arise, since the market quotations for staple commodities and shares of corporations that are traded on the stock exchanges of several countries will be out of

---

to rest at a point of stable equilibrium. An autonomous inflow of funds will, other things being equal, consequently tend to cause appreciation of domestic currency. Profit-maximizing speculators will feel induced to move into the temporarily depreciated foreign currency if markets had been in equilibrium before the disturbance brought about by the capital inflow (see chap. iii below).

[7] See J. Viner, *Studies in the Theory of International Trade* (New York: Harper, 1937), chap. vi; G. Haberler, *The Theory of International Trade* (London: Hodge, 1936), chap. vii; and H. G. Johnson, *International Trade and Economic Growth* (Cambridge, Mass.: Harvard University Press, 1958), chap. vii, also for references to other writings. Professor Johnson distinguishes between two different "transfer problems": first, the question whether an autonomous capital movement will bring about a "real" transfer of goods and services (the classical transfer problem proper); second, the question whether automatic forces will be called into motion to restore equilibrium (p. 170). The existence of fluctuating exchange rates guarantees the solution of the first problem, but not necessarily that of the second. Under full-employment conditions, supporting monetary policy will generally be needed to make depreciation effective (see sec. 4 below).

[ 23 ]

line. It is easily seen that this kind of arbitrage, which can normally be effected at small cost and with little delay, will contribute toward high elasticity of demand and supply of foreign exchange in the very short run. I suspect that this has been one of the principal factors contributing toward the remarkable stability of the Canadian dollar since the official peg for this currency was abandoned in 1950.

While this factor can be expected to succeed in bridging the random disturbances that arise in the foreign-exchange market from hour to hour and from day to day, the volume of transactions of this type is presumably not important enough to smooth out larger disturbances, such as those due to seasonal factors or to the transfer of a large international loan. This task will have to be performed by other means of adjustment. We shall argue in later chapters that foreign-exchange speculation is ideally suited for this purpose and that it can reasonably be expected to perform its task satisfactorily if general economic policy provides a suitable climate. Experience has, I believe, shown convincingly that continuous stabilization of exchange rates by central banks or governmental bodies is a dubious substitute for profit-oriented, private short-term capital movements.[8] I would also argue that complete freedom of capital movements is a *conditio sine qua non* for the success of a system of freely fluctuating exchange rates. Neither the bridging of short-run disparities through international arbitrage between organized exchanges, as described above, nor speculation proper is possible if capital movements are subjected to exchange controls. On the other hand, most authors have argued that flexible exchange rates would not be feasible unless tight controls are imposed on capital movements and all speculative transactions are made impossible.[9]

It will also be demonstrated later in this study how properly guided private speculation and interest arbitrage can be used toward the easier realization of countercyclical objectives. Although

[8] The indorsement of flexible exchange rates in this study should not be misunderstood to imply a summary condemnation of stabilizing central bank intervention in the exchange markets. I am convinced, however, that intelligent guidance of private currency speculation and interest arbitrage by public policy along the lines suggested by the analysis in the following chapters is, barring exceptional circumstances, both sufficient and preferable for safeguarding adequate stability of exchange rates.

[9] See, e.g., S. Laursen and L. Metzler, "Flexible Exchange Rates and the Theory of Employment," *Review of Economics and Statistics*, 32 (1950), 282–83.

these possibilities were hinted at in Keynes's earlier works, they have hardly ever caught the attention of central bankers. These potentially most promising policy tools again presuppose full freedom of capital movements. The detailed discussion of this subject will have to wait until the end of chapter iv.

## 3

### INCOME EFFECTS

"Income effects" of foreign trade properly speaking, i.e., the changes in a country's real national income induced by changes of aggregate demand in foreign countries, are the subject of chapter v. In this section, we shall discuss the effect on a country's national product of autonomous capital movements at initially *given* levels of effective demand in both countries.

There are two different kinds of repercussions of capital movements on the level of output. The first of these is the indirect one due to changes in the volume of credit that may be induced by international capital transfers. It has already been touched upon in our discussion of monetary effects. The second is the direct change in the national income that occurs whenever a capital movement entails a change in the current account of a country's balance of payments. As we have seen, only the first type of adjustment occurs under the gold standard and pegged exchange rates (with the qualification, already pointed out above, that the effects under pegged rates resemble those under fluctuating rates as long as the exchange rate hovers within the gold points or the officially established pegs). Whatever amount of a capital inflow is absorbed by the central bank is not available for the purpose of financing a change in the country's current account. A speculative capital inflow will in the "pure" case of pegged exchange rates immediately boost the central bank's reserves of foreign exchange (or gold) and can only bring about whatever expansionary effect on the country's output an expansion of credit is capable of performing.

The income effects of a capital movement are the exact opposite under a regime of freely fluctuating rates. Assuming that a speculative inflow of funds is not absorbed as an increase in the foreign-exchange portfolios of banks or of "counterspeculators," it must eventually be purchased by commercial traders and will induce additional imports of the same value. A capital inflow is consequently directly *de*flationary under fluctuating exchange rates while it is (indirectly) *in*flationary in the pure case of a regime of pegged exchange rates.[10]

There is a significant difference between the income effects of an imbalance in the current account under pegged and under fluctuating rates. Under orthodox Keynesian assumptions about underemployment "equilibrium," domestic prices are rigid. Stability of exchange rates also means that the prices of all imports remain unchanged over time. When exchange rates are flexible, on the other hand, a capital inflow will not only result in a rise in the value of imports, but also in a reduction of their domestic prices owing to the simultaneous exchange-rate adjustment. In real terms, the increase in imports is consequently larger than suggested by the increase in their value. More important is the fact that the change can generally not remain without influence on domestic prices. The prices of identical goods of domestic origin will have to fall in the same proportion. For other commodities, it is to be expected that there will usually be high enough and predominantly positive cross-elasticities of demand between imports and domestically produced goods so that pressure is brought to bear on most domestic prices.

Having recognized these differences, the question arises next whether the usual repercussions of capital movements under pegged or under fluctuating exchange rates are to be preferred.

*Long-term capital movements* generally respond to real factors and are under normal circumstances relatively independent of expectations concerning short-run movements of exchange rates. Also under normal circumstances (the recent past has, of course, often been anything but normal), countries in which real factors (in particular the marginal productivity of capital) tend to favor long-term capital exports are relatively more likely to suffer from stagnation than countries where real factors favor capital imports. An increased export surplus (or a reduced import surplus, respectively) brought about directly by an outflow of capital under fluctuating exchange rates can therefore, as a rule, be more easily afforded by these countries, as can the cyclical brake of an import surplus by the recipient countries.

By comparison, the generation of the desirable real adjustments in response to an autonomous long-term capital inflow is a round-

[10] This was recognized in G. Haberler, *Prosperity and Depression* (4th ed.; Cambridge, Mass.: Harvard University Press, 1958), chap. xii, pp. 446–48.

about process under the gold standard or pegged exchange rates. To generate an export surplus in the country exporting long-term capital (where stagnation is, as noted above, more likely than in the receiving country), a deflation of credit is brought about and tends to lower effective demand further, whereas the opposite (and, as a rule, inappropriate) cyclical symptoms will be reinforced in the receiving country.

Things look different under universal full-employment conditions. A capital export will, when exchange rates fluctuate freely, provoke neither a contraction of the money supply in the exporting country nor an expansion in the importing country. A "real" transfer still occurs initially, since there are assumed to be no takers but commercial traders for the new supply of foreign exchange in the recipient country, but it has to come about through a depletion of inventories. Unless counteracted by tighter monetary policies, this will eventually lead to price increases in the capital-exporting country. The monetary effects bound to occur when exchange rates are pegged, on the other hand, however important or unimportant they may be, at least tend to work in the right direction. All these relative advantages and disadvantages of the monetary effects and of direct real-income effects of alternative forms of exchange-rate management should not be taken too seriously in any case, since central bankers now rarely consider themselves bound by the forces generated by foreign trade and are most likely to use their own discretion. This should also be borne in mind in the following comparison of advantages with respect to short-term capital movements.

Another qualification is necessary. The term "monetary effects" has so far been used exclusively to denote changes in the quantity of money. Now that direct income effects have been introduced, it will be seen that capital transfers in the "pure" case of fluctuating exchange rates also entail a monetary effect in the form of a tendency toward change in the interest-rate structures of the two countries, even though no change in the volume of money can occur if banks continue to be fully loaned up. This pressure on interest rates comes about through the changes in the transactions-demand for cash after the commodity movement induced by the capital transfer has altered national incomes. It is easily verified that the changes in interest rates go in a direction that tends to re-establish equilibrium.

*Short-term capital transfers* are predominantly guided by specula-

[ 27 ]

tive anticipations of exchange-rate movements. Short-term funds will flow into countries whose currencies are expected to appreciate. *If* all countries pursue policies designed to preserve long-run stability of exchange rates, short-term capital will generally move to countries whose currencies have temporarily depreciated. These will, however, also be the countries where deflationary policies are needed more than elsewhere and where the import surplus generated by a short-term capital inflow is consequently most desirable.

If, on the other hand, a country's policies do *not* promote long-run stability of exchange rates and the price level, the income effects of speculative capital movements under freely fluctuating rates are likely to become self-inflammatory. If depreciation of a currency is under way and is expected to continue, speculative capital will move away. The capital outflow tends to induce additional exports. This must aggravate the inflationary trend to which the depreciation of the currency can be expected to have been due in the first place.

In the "pure" case of truly pegged exchange rates (i.e., where buying and selling rates coincide) nobody is supposed to have any incentive to undertake speculative capital movements. With the normal spread between buying and selling rates, the adjustment processes are the same as under fluctuating rates as long as the rate fluctuates within these limits. When the rate bounces against one of the boundary values, there are two possibilities of speculative behavior. One is that speculators believe that the authorities will succeed in preserving the given peg, in which case the effect of profit-maximizing speculation on the exchange rate will be "stabilizing." It will not, however, have any repercussions on effective demand or the money supply that would speed up the expected adjustment. On the contrary, while direct income effects are again absent, the induced monetary effects go in the *opposite* direction.

The other possibility is that speculators, distrusting the power or the willingness of the authorities to preserve the given peg when the rate has moved to one of the extreme values, undertake "destabilizing" speculation.[11] Direct income effects are again absent since all foreign exchange demanded by speculators will be offered by the central bank when the currency has depreciated to the upper exchange-rate peg. The induced monetary effects, however, go in a

---

[11] The term "destabilizing" is inclosed in quotation marks since its use for *any* action that tends to move a variable away from its previous level may be most inappropriate. See chap. iii, sec. 2 below.

direction that accelerates the return to the previous equilibrium. To summarize these results, it is seen that speculative capital movements by themselves stabilize best (and directly) under *fluctuating* exchange rates when speculators expect long-term *stability*, whereas they tend to stabilize, though in a rather indirect manner, under *pegged* exchange rates when speculators expect that the peg *cannot* be preserved. Given the present unwillingness of most central banks to submit their policies to the dictate of international transactions, too much cannot be expected from induced changes in the money supply alone. Any benefits or disadvantages arising from this source under the alternative forms of exchange-rate management ought to be rather dubious.

On the other hand, the direct income effects of autonomous capital movements, typical of a regime of fluctuating rates, should be quite marked, both when they are desirable and when they are undesirable. From the preliminary evidence of this chapter, a system of freely fluctuating rates, combined with measures designed to establish confidence in their stability over the long run, would appear as the optimal combination. Subsequent chapters will show that this preliminary conclusion seems to stand up well, although it will be seen that valid conclusions are possible only after the complications arising from the existence of forward exchange markets are explored in detail.

Noticeable benefits should also arise from the increased price flexibility which a regime of fluctuating exchange rates forces upon the participating countries. There can be little doubt about the effectiveness of high flexibility of individual prices in preventing structural maladjustments. Although the advantages of price flexibility as a *countercyclical* buffer pose a problem too far outside our main topic to be discussed, let alone solved, here, it would seem that, on balance, flexibility is at least most unlikely to do harm.

In looking at theoretical writings of recent years, one is struck by the relative neglect of monetary factors in discussions of balance-of-payments problems. In the models around which theories were built and on which policy conclusions were often based, real variables have often appeared in a complete monetary vacuum. Monetary policy is usually presented as operating exclusively through adjustments of real national income. Failure to investigate the motivation and the effects of autonomous capital movements makes one liable to overlook the mutual interaction of monetary variables with the direction and magnitude of capital flows. It may already be seen from this chapter that monetary policy is much more likely to be effective through this channel than through the roundabout and relatively slow mechanism of income changes.

4

TERMS-OF-TRADE EFFECTS[12]

*The "classical" transfer problem.*—The criteria for the terms-of-trade change after the completion of a capital transfer will differ depending on whether or not full employment is preserved at all times in the countries involved. The formal criterion for the direction of the terms-of-trade change is particularly simple in the former (the "classical") case.

The terms of trade always change in response to the change in reciprocal demand for the two countries' output. The change in reciprocal demand, in turn, depends on the division of increments of real purchasing power in each country upon each other's products. Under continuous full-employment conditions and in the absence of tariffs and transport costs, the fall in real absorption in the country making the transfer will equal the rise in real absorption in the recipient country.[13] The condition for the terms of trade to remain unchanged in this case is, therefore, that the sum of the proportions of increments in real absorption which the two countries spend on imports should be exactly one.[14] In this case, there is no change in

[12] This is an aspect of capital movements that has been extensively discussed in the literature. See G. Haberler, *The Theory of International Trade* (London: Hodge, 1936), chap. ix; J. Viner, *Studies in the Theory of International Trade* (New York: Harper, 1937), chap. vi; J. E. Meade, *A Geometry of International Trade* (London: Allen & Unwin, 1952), chap. vii; P. A. Samuelson, "The Transfer Problem and Transport Costs," *Economic Journal*, **62** (June, 1952), 278–304 and **64** (June, 1954), 264–89; Johnson, *International Trade and Economic Growth*, chap. vii.

[13] With variable production, an index-number problem arises and the measurement of changes in real expenditure becomes ambiguous. We shall gloss over these difficulties here. The term "absorption" was coined by S. S. Alexander in "Effects of a Devaluation on a Trade Balance," *International Monetary Fund Staff Papers*, **2** (1951–52), 263–78.

[14] Meade calls the proportions of marginal expenditure which are spent on foreign goods the "marginal propensities to import." This is misleading, since the term is usually reserved for the proportions spent on foreign goods of increments of *income*, not expenditure. *Geometry*, p. 86. See also H. G. Johnson, "The Taxonomic Approach to Economic Policy," *Economic Journal*, **61** (1951), 812–32.

[ 30 ]

reciprocal demand, as is easily deduced. If the sum of the proportions is smaller than one, reciprocal demand for the recipient country's goods will increase after the change and the terms of trade will move in its favor. If the sum of the proportions exceeds unity, the terms of trade of the paying country improve.

On purely theoretical grounds, the usual treatment of the classical transfer problem thus establishes no presumption in favor of a deterioration of the terms of trade of the paying country, as had long been taken for granted.[15] The classical presumption is valid, however, to the extent that it can be verified empirically that marginal proportions of expenditure on imports typically average less than one half, and it is reinforced by the existence of tariffs and transport costs.[16] It does not matter, on the other hand, whether production of individual commodities is assumed fixed or variable along a smooth production possibility locus, for all adjustments in production are themselves governed by the final position of the terms of trade.

The traditional treatment of the terms-of-trade aspect of capital transfers, as represented by the contributions of Meade and Samuelson, takes a real transfer of a certain quantity of goods as *given*. It thus dismisses the question of whether an adjustment of relative prices might be needed (perhaps for only a transitory period) to bring about a real transfer of commodities in the first place. The payment of reparations accompanied by simultaneous fiscal measures designed to adjust incomes by the exact amounts required to effect the real transfer is a case that corresponds most closely to the Meade-Samuelson approach. Principal emphasis in this study, on the other hand, is placed on the adjustment processes that follow spontaneous movements of private capital *un*accompanied by fiscal changes. The *ex ante* real value of monetary capital transfers need not be exactly equal to the volume of the *ex post* flow of goods and services. Changes in the absolute price levels in the two countries, in relative prices of individual commodities as well as exchange-rate movements may occur in the interval before the real transfer is completed and prevent exact equality.

This is an appropriate occasion to warn against the identification of changes in exchange rates with changes in the terms of

---

[15] The *locus classicus* is J. S. Mill's *Principles of Political Economy*, Book III, chap. xxi, sec. 4.

[16] Samuelson, "The Transfer Problem and Transport Costs," *op. cit.*

trade.[17] Exchange-rate adjustments primarily affect the relationship between the price levels of different countries, whereas the terms of trade express relative prices of different goods *within* a country. It is by no means intuitively obvious that a change of the exchange rate in a given direction should also lead to a change in relative prices of individual commodities in a certain direction. For the case of an alteration of an (adjustably) pegged exchange rate and given elasticities of supply and demand of exports and imports, Joan Robinson has developed the appropriate criterion. It states that depreciation of a currency will lead to a deterioration of a country's terms of trade whenever the product of the two countries' elasticities of supply of exports exceeds the product of the elasticities of their demands for imports.[18] Under the most extreme assumptions of Keynesian underemployment "equilibrium," supply in both countries is perfectly elastic and the condition is necessarily fulfilled. When full employment is continuously maintained, on the other hand, the matter is more ambiguous.[19]

Let us return to the case of an outflow of funds from a fully employed economy in a system of freely fluctuating exchange rates. The study of the mechanism by which such an outflow can bring about a real export surplus is of obvious relevance to the question of how an export surplus is generated after devaluation.

The first effect of a capital outflow is depreciation of the country's currency. As previous sections of this chapter have shown, an export surplus must follow almost immediately, since commercial traders are the only takers of the new supply of domestic currency if equilibrium had ruled before the change. An increase in exports is possible even under full-employment conditions; in the short run, supply can be fed out of inventories.

[17] For example, devaluation is necessarily held to imply a deterioration in the terms of trade in F. C. Benham, "The Terms of Trade," *Economica*, N.S., 7 (1940), 373; or J. J. Polak and T. C. Chang, "Effect of Exchange Depreciation on a Country's Export Price Level," *Int. Mon. Fund Staff Papers*, 1 (1950–51), 49–70.

[18] J. Robinson, "Beggar-My-Neighbor Remedies for Unemployment," *Essays in the Theory of Employment* (London and New York: Macmillan, 1937), n. 17. The second (1947) edition is reprinted in American Economic Association, *Readings in the Theory of International Trade* (Philadelphia: Blakiston, 1950).

[19] See the contributions listed in F. Machlup, "The Terms-of-Trade Effects of Devaluation upon Real Income and the Balance of Trade," *Kyklos*, 9 (1956), 417–20.

This is only a possibility for the short run, however. The attempt by exporters to replenish their reduced inventories will transmit the initial rise in effective demand to the rest of the economy.

Where unemployment exists, the adjustment to a higher volume of exports (or a reduction of imports) is no problem. Under full-employment conditions, the basic assumption underlying this section, other variables have to be brought into action. The view has been expressed that "at full employment, it is possible to improve the foreign balance only through reducing absorption."[20] Machlup has challenged this view by pointing out that it neglects the possibility of improvements in the allocation of resources following devaluation.[21] The possibility of improving the foreign balance under full-employment conditions while holding the level of domestic absorption (though not its composition) constant lies at the heart of the problem posed in chapter vi below. The significance of this argument can hardly be emphasized enough in view of the fact that many economists and policymakers seem to be unaware of it, although it involves nothing more than an understanding of the principle of comparative advantage. An improvement of the foreign balance through this mechanism is open to a country whenever depreciation of a pegged currency facilitates an improvement in resource allocation which otherwise could not take place. It presupposes the existence of controls on foreign trade whose removal becomes possible after depreciation. Practical experience has shown that such controls are almost invariably imposed before the authorities of a country can be persuaded to devalue an "adjustably pegged" currency. Conclusions based on improved allocation of resources are eminently realistic in that case.

The improvement of the foreign balance through reallocation of fully employed resources is one of the few instances in which the terms of trade of the devaluing country *must* deteriorate.[22] Removal

[20] Alexander, "Effects of a Devaluation on a Trade Balance," p. 274.

[21] F. Machlup, "Relative Prices and Aggregate Spending in the Analysis of Devaluation," *American Economic Review*, 45 (1955), 255–78, and "The Terms-of-Trade Effects of Devaluation upon Real Income and the Balance of Trade," *Kyklos*, 9 (1956), 417–52. Johnson's otherwise excellent summary of the absorption approach is marred by his lack of emphasis on changes in resource allocation. "Towards a General Theory of the Balance of Payments," chap. vi of *International Trade and Economic Growth*.

[22] Another case in which the terms of trade have to deteriorate after devaluation occurs when the foreign-exchange market is statically unstable. See G.

of controls on foreign trade induces producers to specialize more in those commodities in which the country has a comparative advantage. The relative prices of its export commodities in the rest of the world will necessarily tend to fall. Since most devaluations in recent history have been accompanied by a removal of trade restrictions and factor reallocation as indicated above, the layman's instinctive identification of depreciation with a deterioration of the terms of trade appears to be better founded than theorists have generally believed. It would, of course, be more correct to say that the change in the terms of trade is due to the relaxation of controls rather than to the devaluation itself. It is particularly true in this case, moreover, that the resulting deterioration of the terms of trade is more likely to benefit than to hurt the country. The controls designed to check a disequilibrium in a country's balance of payments have to be imposed on top of its existing structure of tariffs and quotas and will probably push protection beyond what might be the ambiguously defined "optimum" degree in the majority of cases.[23]

Depreciation of a currency in a *free* exchange market, on the other hand, precludes the feasibility of improvements in the allocation of resources as a result of the depreciation alone. Given full employment, an improvement in the foreign balance following depreciation can then indeed come about only through a reduction in domestic absorption. Of the two principal tools available for this purpose, fiscal and monetary policy, the effectiveness of the former is generally acknowledged. A decrease in government spending or a reduction of consumption after an increase in taxes frees resources and makes possible a rise in the production of exports without any further ado. The only, but devastating, objection to fiscal policy is that it is too sluggish and awkward a tool for the purpose discussed here, the achievement of a real transfer after any spontaneous (and therefore generally unpredictable) movement of long- or short-term capital in a free exchange market.

Under our assumptions, the achievement of a real export surplus after an autonomous capital outflow through supporting monetary

---

Haberler, "Currency Depreciation and the Terms of Trade," in *Wirtschaftliche Entwicklung und soziale Ordnung* (Vienna: Herold, 1952), pp. 149 ff. This situation is only possible if the exchange rate is pegged, as chap. i has shown.

[23] See the Appendix for details.

policy, though generally acknowledged as a measure that can be undertaken with little delay, requires greater effectiveness of monetary policy than it is widely credited with nowadays. Since we want to retain our basic postulate of full employment, an induced reduction of absorption through a contraction of real national income is precluded. In our framework, monetary policy is allowed to liberate resources only through whatever changes in investment and consumption out of a *given* real income interest rates are capable of achieving. The historical evidence that autonomous capital outflows supported by monetary measures, but unaccompanied by fiscal changes, have usually led to a real transfer in a relatively smooth and painless manner and without significant fluctuations in employment is evidence that saving and investment appear to be (or at least used to be) sufficiently interest-elastic according to the classical presumption. This is of profound significance in view of the currently widespread view that saving and investment, and especially the former, respond hardly at all to changes in interest rates.[24]

In all the cases in which a real transfer is generated exclusively through a reduction of domestic absorption by fiscal or monetary means, there is no definite presumption as to the most probable movement of the terms of trade.

The possibilities listed above and variants of essentially the same forces exhaust all the ways in which an improvement of the foreign balance can be brought about under full-employment conditions. Before discussing a few analytical pitfalls the investigator is liable to encounter, I would like to call attention to two related points concerning the operation of the gold standard. The first is the fact that the customary distinction between "pure price" and "pure income" effects which supposedly co-operated in the adjustment process is somewhat oversimplified. The slightest interest-elasticity of saving or investment in the direction presumed by classical economic theory will make possible changes in the foreign balance through the "direct" absorption effects[25] sketched above without necessitating a change either in real income and employment *or* in prices.

[24] See, e.g., L. R. Klein, "The Empirical Foundations of Keynesian Economics," in *Post-Keynesian Economics* (New Brunswick: Rutgers University Press, 1956), p. 292.

[25] Alexander's terminology in "Effects of a Devaluation on a Trade Balance."

Second, "pure" price effects provoked by gold flows cannot by themselves result in an improvement in the foreign balance. Let us consider a capital outflow sufficiently large to move the exchange rate to the gold-export point, for example. The loss of gold and the resulting monetary contraction will, provided prices are flexible enough, eventually lead to a fall of domestic prices. As currently interpreted, the consensus among classical economists was that this alone would suffice to improve the foreign balance by stimulating additional exports and discouraging imports.[26] It is evident, however, that under continuous full employment and with no leeway for a more efficient allocation of resources this is again only possible when the community is willing to reduce its real absorption.[27] Only an increase in the propensity to save or a fall of investment in response to the rise in interest rates after the gold outflow can achieve the required effect. As need hardly be added, governments did not consciously practice functional finance in the modern sense during the reign of the gold standard.

It has already been pointed out that, if changes in interest rates are capable of affecting absorption in this way, neither price nor income effects in the traditional sense are necessary for an improvement of the balance of payments. In fact, the attempt to explain balance-of-payments adjustment through the "price effects" envisaged by the classical economists runs into serious difficulties that do not seem to have been pointed out before. The fall of prices in the gold-exporting country that was supposed to attract foreign buyers attracts domestic buyers as well. To the extent that it does, it would at first sight already seem to work against an improvement of the foreign balance. The fall of the domestic price level also implies a fall of aggregate money income in the same proportion, however (neglecting the index-number problem that obviously arises if not all prices change in the same proportion). No change in aggregate real income has consequently taken place.[28] On the other hand,

[26] Cf. Mill, *Principles of Political Economy*, Book III, chap. xxi.

[27] The contraction of domestic absorption need not be instantaneous. Inventories may act as a shock absorber.

[28] In the real world, not all prices will usually change in the same proportion. It might be thought that movements of sectional price levels at home and abroad can bring about a fall of domestic real income and a subsequent reduction in absorption. Any fall in real income through this mechanism presupposes a deterioration of the country's terms of trade. As will be pointed out below, the

the fall of domestic prices implies a positive (though presumably weak) real-balance effect.[29] In the absence of further information, we would still expect an increase rather than constancy or a fall of real domestic absorption. We thus reach the inevitable conclusion that, under continued full-employment conditions and in the absence of direct absorption effects of interest-rate changes, the classical price effects of a gold outflow alone work *against* the required adjustment in the foreign balance. The smoothness of the transfer process under the gold standard that puzzled Taussig and his students must be interpreted as convincing evidence of the effectiveness of the direct absorption effects of interest-rate changes and thus of sufficiently high interest-elasticity of saving and investment.[30]

It might be objected that the classical assumption of full employment was unrealistic anyway and that it was always income effects that guaranteed smooth adjustment. As shown below (chap.

---

over-all effect of an unfavorable movement of the terms of trade is to make the adjustment problem even *more* difficult.

[29] The real-balance effect is less straightforward in this case than would appear at first sight. The fall of prices after a gold outflow comes about through a monetary contraction. The public thus holds fewer balances whose real value could increase. The crudest version of the quantity theory would imply that the aggregate real value of the money supply can *never* change, irrespective of the nominal quantity of money in circulation at any time. A positive real-balance effect can then come about only through the change in the real value of outstanding government bonds. The increase of the latter which is due to a fall in the price level has to be corrected for the effect of the accompanying rise in interest rates on the market value of bonds. The former will dominate unless the bulk of the government debt is funded in very long-term issues. On the whole, the real-balance effect is probably not very significant for the issue under review.

[30] The leading studies are J. H. Williams, *Argentine International Trade under Inconvertible Paper Money, 1880–1900* (Cambridge, Mass.: Harvard University Press, 1920); J. Viner, *Canada's Balance of International Indebtedness, 1900–1913* (Cambridge, Mass.: Harvard University Press, 1924); F. W. Taussig, *International Trade* (New York: Macmillan, 1927), esp. chaps. xx–xxv; J. W. Angell, "Equilibrium in International Trade: The U.S. 1919–26," *Quarterly Journal of Economics*, **42** (1928), 388–433; A. G. Silverman, "Some International Trade Factors for Great Britain," *Review of Economic Statistics*, **13** (1931), 114–24; H. D. White, *The French International Accounts, 1880–1913* (Cambridge, Mass.: Harvard University Press, 1933). For an excellent survey of this series of investigations, see White, pp. 3–35. The inability of traditional doctrine to explain the surprising ease of adjustment in most of these cases is well characterized by Taussig's conclusion that "... things just *happened* so ..." (p. 332, italics in the original).

iii, sec. 3), this claim is untenable, since Keynesian income effects are sure to be very sluggish.

Our insistence on the fact that changes in price levels *alone* cannot serve as a means of improving the balance on current account should not be misunderstood to imply that price changes have no role to play at all. If they did not, neither would movements of exchange rates have any function to perform. After a given disturbance, such as an autonomous capital movement, there will generally be new equilibrium values of all prices and exchange rates. The necessary role of price changes in a smoothly functioning system is evident, since maladjustment must result if any price is artificially prevented from moving to the new equilibrium level.

Price-level changes may be particularly important as catalysts and signals in the dynamic adjustment process to the new equilibrium. If domestic prices in both countries are temporarily constant, the first reaction to a capital outflow and the induced currency depreciation is likely to be a switch of expenditure toward the commodities of the capital-exporting country. Unless the flow of capital produces an *instantaneous* contraction of domestic demand in the country where it originates and an instantaneous expansion of domestic demand elsewhere, the first result of the expenditure switch is a tendency for domestic prices to rise in the former and to fall in the latter. If the monetary authorities are committed to the preservation of price stability, they will automatically take the necessary measures to adjust absorption in the directions required to achieve the real transfer, even though the capital movement does not by itself produce the usual monetary effects.

Though changes in price levels played a role in the sequence of events sketched above, it will be noted that they were the *opposite* of those described in the classical version. Yet the chain of causation appears eminently realistic.[31]

There is an important asymmetry between the paying and the receiving country. Under full-employment conditions, the paying country can achieve an export surplus only by reducing its absorption, and it was shown above that a fall of its price level cannot, by

---

[31] The present example needs additional qualification. It was assumed that the exchange rate was free to adjust in the required direction, a condition that would not be fulfilled if the rate had originally been at the gold-export point (from the point of view of the capital-exporting country). Changes in absorption are then the only mechanism of adjustment, even in the short run.

itself, bring about this effect. For the receiving country, on the other hand, a general fall of prices abroad (assuming constant exchange rates) is well capable of increasing its demand for imports from the rest of the world without any help from its monetary authorities. The expenditure switch toward imported commodities, to the extent that adjustments in the rest of the world can make it effective, will result in a roughly equal fall of effective demand for domestic goods. There is no natural barrier to a *fall* of the national output below the full-employment level, as there is to a rise above it.

Another aspect of the asymmetry concerns the effect of an autonomous *rise* of domestic prices in a country. Although we found that a uniform proportional *fall* of all prices cannot, by itself, generate an *export* surplus,[32] a uniform *rise* of a country's prices can bring about an *import* surplus simultaneously with a fall of demand for home products and the associated effects on the real national product. These are the typical phenomena associated with "cost-push" inflation under pegged exchange rates. The proposal to fight the stagnation customarily associated with cost-push inflation with more demand inflation overlooks the adverse effects on the employment level of the induced deterioration in the external balance. The net effect on the employment level remains entirely uncertain.

A variant of the direct absorption effects discussed above is the following sequence of events. The loss of gold by the capital-exporting country may engender expectations of a fall of prices in the near future. Even with momentarily constant nominal interest rates, such expectations amount to a rise in the *real* rate of interest. The rise may be very steep if the fall of prices is expected very shortly. Provided that saving and investment are interest-elastic according to the classical presumption, real absorption will fall and facilitate a real transfer abroad.

Modern writers often identify Keynesian income effects with the "shifts in purchasing power" which some pre-Keynesian writers had pointed out as an important variable of adjustment.[33] There is hardly any doubt, however, that most of the earlier writers had something un-Keynesian in mind: a change in domestic absorption with *unchanged* real income, the phenomenon we were presently

[32] Except through a temporary reduction of inventories.

[33] E.g., W. M. Scammell, *International Monetary Policy* (London: Macmillan, 1957), p. 34, n. 1.

discussing.[34] Such a change is, to be sure, not in conflict with the Keynesian mold of thinking if it is brought about by fiscal measures. What post-Keynesians usually find hard to swallow is the idea that purely monetary phenomena can bring about such changes of significant magnitude. It should also be pointed out that the pre-Keynesian authors who emphasized shifts in purchasing power (for example, Ohlin and White) did not always make clear what their interpretations imply. To a casual reader, it might appear as if they would take it for granted that a mere transfer of funds between banks in different countries is equivalent to a transfer of purchasing power. Successful adjustment, however, requires effects of such transfers on *real* variables whose existence is by no means universally recognized, at least not under full-employment conditions.

To demonstrate the feasibility of an improvement of the balance on current account through depreciation while the terms of trade remain constant, the device of dividing all commodities into "international" and "domestic" ones has been employed. The latter group comprises those goods which customarily do not move across national boundaries.[35] One possibility of effecting the real transfer was emphasized by Taussig and indorsed by Graham and Viner: a fall in the price of "domestic" commodities relative to prices of both imports and exports in the transferring country (and vice versa in the receiving country).[36] Such a change, it was held, diverts expenditure in the transferring country toward home goods and liberates more of the "international" commodities for export. This solution again presupposes the existence of unused resources and is not feasible under full-employment conditions. A diversion of expenditure toward domestic goods also diverts resources there and

[34] This is certainly true of the nineteenth-century writers reviewed in Viner's *Studies*, pp. 300–304. Neither does Ohlin's analysis, both in his controversy with Keynes on the German reparations problem and in *Interregional and International Trade* (Cambridge, Mass.: Harvard University Press, 1933), convey the impression that he thought of adjustments in the level of real income and employment.

[35] See Viner, *Studies*, pp. 323–ff.

[36] *Ibid.* See also F. W. Taussig, "International Trade under Depreciated Paper," *Quarterly Journal of Economics*, Vol. 31 (1917); F. D. Graham, "International Trade under Depreciated Paper: The United States, 1862–1879," *Quarterly Journal of Economics*, 36 (1922), 227–73; J. Viner, *Canada's Balance of International Indebtedness 1900–1913* (Cambridge, Mass.: Harvard University Press, 1924), chap. ix.

leaves that much less for the production of export goods if no resources are idle.[37]

None of the cases we have discussed involves a change in the terms of trade, except the one where the improvement in the foreign balance comes about through reallocation of a given quantity of factors toward lines of comparative advantage. On the other hand, we recognized that case as the one of greatest practical importance in the devaluation of an adjustably pegged exchange rate. The question arises whether deterioration of the terms of trade can, other things being given, itself contribute toward an improvement of the foreign balance. One might be tempted to argue that, because a fall in the terms of trade at a given level of money income and employment implies a reduction of real national income, it must induce a fall of imports and thus lead to an improvement of the balance on current account. As Alexander has pointed out, this reasoning overlooks the fact that any worsening of the terms of trade has the immediate consequence of causing a deterioration of the money value (in terms of foreign currency) of the trade balance for given physical quantities of exports and imports. Alexander shows that the fall of imports induced by the reduction in real income can under the usual assumptions never fully compensate for the adverse primary effect. Whatever deterioration of the terms of trade occurs therefore only makes the adjustment problem more difficult.[38] By the same token,

[37] There is an obvious slip in Meade's reasoning that there will be a "shift of demand . . . from foreign-trade to home-trade products and of supply in the *reverse* direction." *The Balance of Payments* (London: Oxford University Press, 1951), p. 234 (my italics).

[38] "Effects of a Devaluation on a Trade Balance," pp. 268–69. Assume that a certain deterioration of the terms of trade makes the balance on current account deteriorate by $t$ units of real income for *given* physical quantities of exports and imports. A fall in domestic absorption by $t$ units is therefore required in order merely to forestall a worsening of the foreign balance. The unfavorable movement of the terms of trade also lowers real income by $t$ units. With a marginal propensity to spend of $c$, a fall in absorption by $c \times t$ units follows. This is less than the reduction in absorption required to compensate for the adverse primary effect on the foreign balance whenever $c < 1$. To the extent that real income admits of unambiguous measurement, and if improvements of resource allocation are ruled out, Alexander's argument is unexceptionable.

The conclusions of this section are of obvious relevance to the famous reparations controversy. J. M. Keynes, "The German Transfer Problem," and B. Ohlin, "The Reparation Problem," *Economic Journal*, **39** (1929), 1–7, 172–73, reprinted in American Economic Association, *Readings in the Theory of International Trade*, (Philadelphia: Blakiston, 1950), pp. 161–78.

[ 41 ]

the improvement in the foreign balance is facilitated if devaluation happens to lead to an *improvement* in the terms of trade.

Since the fall of real income in the case discussed above is due to a change in *prices* while employment is assumed to remain constant, we are within the confines of the "classical" transfer problem. Some doubt arises whether a treatment in terms of Keynesian marginal propensities, the method employed by Alexander, is at all permissible here. John Spraos has emphasized that there is no reason to believe that marginal propensities to consume are the same whether the change in real national income is brought about by price-level or by employment changes.[39] The issue under review involves only the rather general question of whether the marginal propensity to spend is between zero and one, however, and should be relatively immune to this objection.

Among other ways of achieving an improvement in the foreign balance through direct absorption effects, the real-balance effect of a rise in the domestic price level and the possibility of money illusion may be listed for completeness, but hardly as more than mere curiosities.[40]

*The "Keynesian" transfer problem.*—The relaxation of the full-employment assumption considerably complicates the formal criteria for the terms-of-trade changes after transfers. Owing to the existence of multiplier effects, the final changes in the two countries' real incomes may not be the same even when the primary changes in real aggregate demand occasioned by a transfer are equal in absolute amount, a condition which will usually not be fulfilled either. The originators of the Keynesian approach to the transfer problem established one notable difference between the formal terms-of-trade criteria in the "classical" and in the "Keynesian" cases: whereas the direction of changes in the terms of trade after the completion of the transfer was ambiguous in the former case, as outlined above, the answer in the latter proved to be that the terms-of-trade change is always unfavorable for the transferring country as long as the marginal propensities to save in both countries are positive.[41] Professor Johnson has pointed out that this result is actually

[39] J. Spraos, "Consumers' Behavior and the Conditions for Exchange Stability," *Economica*, N.S., 22 (1955), 137–47.

[40] Alexander, "Effects of a Devaluation on a Trade Balance," pp. 271–73.

[41] L. A. Metzler, "The Transfer Problem Reconsidered," *Journal of Political Economy*, Vol. 50 (1942), reprinted in *Readings in the Theory of International*

due to a few special simplifying assumptions made by Metzler and Machlup.[42]

We shall not pursue the analysis of the Keynesian transfer problem any further. One reason is that there is every indication that the "Keynesian" variety of unemployment is hardly a live problem any more. Future generations of economists may well come to regard the emphasis on macroeconomics of the post-Keynesian type in current teaching and research as one of the frequent instances in which economists have applied themselves predominantly to the solution of problems of the past. The fact that the nature of economic recessions caused by a shortage of effective demand is no longer a riddle to theorists does not, of course, imply that policymakers can be relied upon to know the answers and always to act accordingly. Competent popularizers are needed as urgently as ever before. I would not, however, count post-Keynesian economics among the fields in which the marginal returns of further theoretical refinements are very high in terms of the insight to be gained for the conduct of policy. The possibility of non-cyclical varieties of economic stagnation, among which the behavior of the United States economy in recent years would undoubtedly have to be classified, cannot be denied. This may well turn out to be our major policy problem in years to come, and one that may prove to be much less tractable than simple Keynesian unemployment, owing to greater institutional resistance to its cure. In spite of widespread disagreement with this view, I would venture the opinion that Keynesian tools are more likely to obscure than to illuminate the real nature of the trouble. There is all the less reason to dwell extensively on national-income models in this study since the task of counter-cyclical policy is considerably simplified in an environment of flexible exchange rates, as the following chapters should make amply clear.

---

*Trade*, pp. 179–97; F. Machlup, *International Trade and the National Income Multiplier* (Philadelphia: Blakiston, 1943), chap. ix.

[42] H. G. Johnson, "The Reparations Problem: A Correction," *Economic Journal*, 63 (1953), 724–25, and *International Trade and Economic Growth*, pp. 179–83. See also M. C. Kemp, "Unilateral Transfers and the Terms of Trade," *American Economic Review*, 46 (1956), 106–27. Kemp's treatment is also marred by the assumption that "total spending out of a given money income is invariant under changes in the prices of imported and home-produced commodities" (109, also 120). This is in conflict with Keynesian assumptions, as shown in chap. v below.

Apart from these more practical considerations, the national-income approach is, apart from a brief excursion in chapter v, de-emphasized in this study also for purely theoretical reasons. Keynesian tools reveal their intrinsic weaknesses perhaps more clearly when they are applied to problems of international trade than for any other use. Of the various concepts that are commonly applied, the "marginal propensity to import" is probably the least satisfactory one. It is not even clear what the *dimension* of the marginal propensity to import ought to be.[43] Already for a two-commodity world and extreme price rigidity of domestically produced commodities, the units of measurement of real imports as well as of their value are ambiguous when exchange rates are flexible. The concept of "real income" is, moreover, not clearly definable in that case. The combination of the various possibilities of defining imports and real income yields a number of "marginal propensities to import," none of which has self-evident claims to being the most natural one. It is easy to convince oneself, furthermore, that the assumption of constancy of *any* one of these marginal propensities even for given values of real national income (however defined) will generally conflict with basic norms of economic behavior whenever flexibility of exchange rates is admitted. Reallocation of demand between imports and domestic goods at given levels of real income is, after all, the basic function of exchange-rate adjustment. Marginal import propensities will inevitably be affected by variations of exchange rates. To employ a rubber concept of this kind in more elaborate models, however widespread that practice may be at this stage, seems of little use unless only very general properties of marginal propensities are needed. It is equally defensible in this latter case to employ appropriately defined "total" elasticities of demand for imports instead.[44] This practice will be followed throughout most of this study.

[43] M. Shinohara, "The Multiplier and the Marginal Propensity to Import," *American Economic Review*, **47** (1957), 608–24. The Keynesian contributions to the theory of international trade are also criticized in chap. iv of J. M. Letiche's *Balance of Payments and Economic Growth* (New York: Harper, 1959).

[44] See chap. i above.

# III

## *Motivation and Effects of Speculation in Foreign Exchange*

### 1

### MONOPOLISTIC AND COMPETITIVE SPECULATION

This chapter presents a rough sketch rather than a self-contained and exhaustive theory of speculation. A few radically simplified assumptions will be retained throughout most of it. We shall assume that individual speculators attempt to maximize profits. As usual, this hypothesis is not meant to imply that speculators will always succeed in this endeavor or that they will never deviate from the attempt to reap maximum profits. For purposes of theoretical analysis straight and simple hypotheses are needed to derive meaningful results, unless we want to limit ourselves to the modest but sterile function of telling a bewildered world that almost anything is equally possible in a given situation and that economic reasoning cannot even establish a presumption, with some degree of confidence, that certain outcomes are more likely than others.[1]

---

[1] As an example of the confusion that must befall the practitioner without any guidance from economic theory, Professor Meade, with the assistance of Professor Baumol, has gone to the trouble of calculating the number of possible policy combinations in various simple models of international trade. In one instance, this number was found to be 28,781,143,379. J. E. Meade, *The Balance of Payments: Mathematical Supplement* (London: Oxford University Press, 1951), p. 33, n. 1.

To justify the treatment of speculation in this chapter, I can do no better than to quote Milton Friedman: "Truly important and significant hypotheses will be found to have 'assumptions' that are wildly inaccurate descriptive representations of reality. . . . A hypothesis is important if it 'explains' much by

The lifeblood of speculation in foreign exchange is the tendency of floating exchange rates to vary over time. In this chapter we again consider only spot markets. Let us first suppose that speculators correctly foresee the future path of the rate.[2] This can never be a perfectly valid postulate, of course. Hindsight will always reveal that speculators have, at best, only been approximately correct. As emphasized before, however, hypotheses of one kind or another are necessary for unambiguous conclusions; and this one appears to be more easily defensible than the alternative hypothesis that the rational, profit-maximizing speculator is always mistaken. We would have to suppose in the latter case, furthermore, that he persistently and tirelessly continues to commit the same type of error time and again, for only that would provide a mode of behavior from which definite conclusions can be deduced.

In contrast to our assumption, the presence of uncertainty is an essential ingredient of speculative markets in the real world. Speculators' expectations of future events are never exact. At best, they can be described by a probability distribution at each moment in time. Loosely speaking, our approach applies the basic idea of maximum-likelihood estimation: speculators are assumed to act on the basis of distributions that maximize the likelihood of the observed outcome. The omission of stochastic elements may be regarded as a major shortcoming. Those aspects of speculative activity that are of principal interest for our purposes and which are themselves widely misunderstood are brought out more clearly by a non-stochastic treatment, however. The investigation of speculators' behavior under perfect foresight will make us appreciate the advantages of governmental policies that guarantee a high degree of predictability. It should not let us forget, on the other hand, that it would be folly to rely on the assumption that all governments have recognized these advantages and act accordingly. Nor can we suppose, a posteriori, that speculators will behave as if foresight were highly accurate whenever we know that it cannot be.

---

little, that is, if it abstracts the common and crucial elements from the mass of complex and detailed circumstances surrounding the phenomena to be explained and permits valid predictions on the basis of them alone" (*Essays in Positive Economics* [Chicago: University of Chicago Press, 1953], p. 14).

[2] The same basic assumption is made in a recent contribution by P. A. Samuelson, "Intertemporal Price Equilibrium: A Prologue to the Theory of Speculation," *Weltwirtschaftliches Archiv*, **79** (1957), 181–219.

We shall first discuss the simplest possible case in which interest rates in the two countries under consideration are the same (so that speculators are, as far as interest earnings are concerned, indifferent as to where they keep their funds) and in which the exchange rate follows a sinusoidal path of constant amplitude, phase, and period over time in the absence of speculation (such as the oscillation of greatest amplitude in Fig. 4). These assumptions are made merely for convenience of exposition and can easily be relaxed without affecting the substance of the argument.

Suppose there exists one single speculator, and that he is important enough to exercise an influence on the exchange rate and has command over a sufficient supply of funds to undertake the activities described below.

With a given pattern of supply and demand for foreign exchange from non-speculative sources, the exchange rate[3] is a function of time and the intensity of speculative supply of foreign exchange to the market at every instant of time, $s(t)$ (negative values of $s(t)$ indicate speculative purchases):

$$r = r(t, s), \quad \text{where, for stability}, \quad \frac{\partial r}{\partial s} < 0 ; \quad (1)$$

i.e., increased supply of foreign exchange by the monopolistic speculator causes a fall in its price (a depreciation of foreign currency).

If we assume, to simplify matters, that the speculator's operations are costless, his net revenue during a small time interval will be

$$r(t, s) \cdot s(t) \, dt , \quad (2)$$

and over a whole cycle it is

$$\int_0^{2\pi/\omega} r(t, s) \cdot s(t) \, dt , \quad (3)$$

if

$$r_{\{s=0\}} = A \cdot \cos(\omega t + \epsilon) + R \quad \text{(where } \omega, \epsilon \ldots. \text{ parameters)} \quad (4)$$

expresses the basic oscillation in the absence of speculation. Net revenue equals profits if the speculator's foreign-exchange position at the end of the cycle is the same as that at the beginning of the cycle, i.e., if

$$\int_0^{2\pi/\omega} s(t) \, dt = 0 . \quad (5)$$

[3] We retain the previous definition according to which $r$ is the unit price of foreign currency.

[ 47 ]

It is possible to evaluate speculators' profits only if this condition is fulfilled. A book profit on accumulated inventories due to a price rise over the cycle may be wholly spurious since the price might fall back to the original level or even below it if the accumulated inventories were liquidated.[4]

If $s(t) = 0$ over the whole length of the cycle, i.e., if the speculator does not intervene in the market at all, his net revenue is zero. It will also be zero when the speculator's supply function $s(t)$ is such that the exchange rate is at all times equal to $R$, the average level of the fluctuation (Fig. 4). Since his sales of foreign exchange depress its price and his purchases raise it, this result follows when

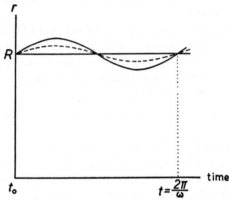

FIG. 4.—Time paths of the exchange rate without speculation (*solid curve*) and with profit-maximizing speculation under accurate foresight (*dashed curve*).

he purchases relatively large amounts during one half of the cycle and sells them during the other half. He can make positive profits by selling and buying only moderate quantities. One of the theorems of the mean[5] guarantees that there is at least one intermediate path

[4] See L. G. Telser, "A Theory of Speculation Relating Profitability and Stability," *Review of Economics and Statistics*, **41** (1959), 295–301, who justly criticizes Baumol's models of speculative markets for leaving this consideration out of account (see also below). Telser's article develops the approach outlined in this section in considerably greater technical detail. It is undoubtedly the most accomplished contribution on speculation presently available. An earlier classic is N. Kaldor's "Speculation and Economic Stability," *Review of Economic Studies*, **7** (1939), 1–27.

[5] Cf. R. G. D. Allen, *Mathematical Analysis for Economists* (London: Macmillan, 1938), p. 452, n. 2.

between maximum fluctuation and perfect stability (such as the broken one in Fig. 4) that yields maximum profits for the speculator.

Mathematically, the task is to find the function $\hat{s}(t)$ that makes the integral in (3) above a maximum, subject to the constraint (5). This is a typical problem in the calculus of variations.[6] Having found the maximizing function $\hat{s}(t)$ (provided the function $r(t, s)$ was known), the time path that results when the monopolistic speculator maximizes profits could be obtained by substitution into $r(t, s)$. The function $r(t, s)$ can, of course, never be known exactly. The calculation of $\hat{s}(t)$ is therefore impossible in the real world. But the effect of maximizing behavior when the speculator's foresight is approximately correct is clear enough: it will reduce the amplitude of fluctuation and hence act in a *stabilizing* manner according to any acceptable definition of stabilizing behavior.[7]

What happens when speculation is not monopolistic, but perfectly competitive? Straightforward application of the traditional classical model would suggest that, if none of the speculators has a perceptive influence on the price of foreign exchange and entry is free, their attempt at profit-maximization will tend to wipe out all profits. Let us again assume that speculators' operations are costless. Given the simple sinusoidal oscillation in (4) above, we are led to the conclusion that perfect competition among speculators with free entry must eliminate all fluctuation entirely and result in a constant exchange rate equal to $R$. For if even a small residual of the original cyclic time path remained, some scope for positive profits of newly entering speculators would exist, contrary to the condition for long-run equilibrium in a perfectly competitive industry.

In the real world, the operations of speculators are not costless. Free entry will eliminate profits while some oscillation still remains. The same is true if entry is not entirely free, possibly because the required volume of freely movable funds is not available or because governments refuse to permit speculative capital movements. Uncertainty is another reason why oscillations will never be entirely eliminated.

[6] Cf. e.g., R. Courant, *Differential and Integral Calculus* (revised ed.; New York: Nordemann, 1940), Vol. 2, chap. vii.

[7] It may perhaps appear a little surprising at first sight that, given smooth functions, profit maximization requires a monopoly speculator to start buying before the price has fallen to its lowest level, and to begin selling at a time when the price is still rising, even though he foresees the future correctly. Such behavior would be precluded under perfectly competitive conditions.

No definite conjecture is possible if speculators' foresight is substantially less than perfect. Governments can contribute to such a state of affairs by confused and erratic policies. The early 1930's provide a classical example. Let us recall that economists then found it difficult to agree on whether inflationary or deflationary policies would more effectively stimulate employment, that nobody could be entirely sure if and when the remaining gold-standard currencies might disappear, or what kind of monetary policies would replace them. It is hardly surprising that nothing anywhere near perfect foresight could be expected from speculators under these conditions.[8]

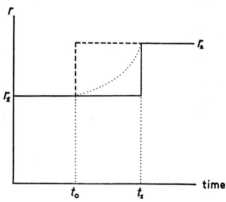

Fig. 5.—Discontinuous jump of the long-run equilibrium rate of exchange from $r_1$ to $r_2$ in the absence of speculation (*solid line*) and with profit-maximizing speculation under varying degrees of accuracy of foresight.

We shall conclude the present section with another special case. Let us suppose that the long-run equilibrium rate of a currency had been at $r_1$ for some time (Fig. 5). At time $t_1$, an event occurs that boosts the rate to the new long-run equilibrium level $r_2$. Speculators possessing advance knowledge or correct anticipation of the event can realize a profit by buying foreign exchange at the lower rate in order to sell at a time when the new rate has been established. If foresight is perfect, they will not stop buying as long as the rate is

[8] The *locus classicus* on the monetary disturbances of the interwar period is League of Nations, *International Currency Experience* (New York: Columbia University Press, 1944). Most of the book is the work of the late Ragnar Nurkse. Tables of exchange-rate movements of the major currencies from 1921 to 1936 can be found in the Appendix of P. Einzig's *Theory of Forward Exchange* (London: Macmillan, 1937).

[ 50 ]

lower. With free entry, equilibrium cannot exist unless the differential is wiped out entirely. If all speculators learn about the expected rise to the new long-run equilibrium level simultaneously at time $t_0$, let us say, the rise that would normally occur at $t_1$ will come about instantly and the time path will be that indicated by the broken line.

The stabilizing effect of profit-maximizing speculation may not be very conspicuous here. A jump that would come about anyway merely occurs a little earlier. What really matters, however, is that competitive speculation again adjusts the price to the new equilibrium level, the only relevant one, with maximum speed. This is the essential function performed by competitive speculation. The "smoothing function" is a necessary consequence of the former only as long as no abrupt and irreversible adjustments occur in the real forces that dominate the market.

Since foresight is never perfect in the real world, not all speculators will usually act at the same instant. If their intervention is randomly distributed over time, a smooth adjustment path such as, for example, the dotted one in Figure 5 will generally result.

It should also be stressed that the actual market rate attains the higher level only if it is expected to persist indefinitely, or for a long enough time period to be considered permanent for all practical purposes. The future downward movement has to be sufficiently uncertain for the exchange rate to rise at all; otherwise, the presence of a field of perfectly competitive speculators with free entry and costless operations guarantees perfect stability, as was shown above.

2

## "STABILIZING" AND "DESTABILIZING" SPECULATION

The concept of stability relevant here, as in most economic considerations, is what Professor Samuelson has called "stability of the first kind."[9] It is displayed by a dynamic system if, after a disturbance, all variables tend to return toward their static equilibrium values as time progresses. The previous section demonstrated that under favorable circumstances perfectly competitive speculation with free entry guarantees a high degree of stability. In-

[9] P. A. Samuelson, *Foundations of Economic Analysis* (Cambridge, Mass.: Harvard University Press, 1947), p. 261.

deed, if operations were costless and foresight were perfect, the exchange rate would never deviate from its long-run equilibrium value *as long as this value does not change itself.*

The qualification in italics is of the utmost importance, for a mistaken notion of "stability" has crept into the discussion of flexible exchanges: the idea that perfect stability implies *constancy* of the nominal rate of exchange between currencies. With this idea in mind, any tendency of speculation (or, for that matter, even of the evolution of normal commercial trade) to move the rate away from a given value is liable to be called "destabilizing." Speculation can legitimately be called destabilizing only if it induces a movement away from the *equilibrium* value or values. It should be obvious that myriads of factors may cause a change in the equilibrium value itself. Whenever speculation causes pressure on the *actual* rate of exchange—which may be held at some arbitrary value by the intervention of a stabilization agency or by straightforward government decree—to follow such a movement or to anticipate it, it must be called *stabilizing* and not destabilizing speculation. A reappraisal of the history of exchange-rate fluctuations between World Wars I and II, familiar from Ragnar Nurkse's painstaking account,[10] might reveal that speculation has been stabilizing more often than would appear at first.[11]

A superficial reading of certain passages in Hicks's *Value and Capital*[12] could convey the impression that he is guilty of the misconception pointed out here. Hicks's "elasticity of expectation" of the price of commodity $X$ is defined as "the ratio of the proportional rise in expected future prices of $X$ to the proportional rise in its current price."[13] Zero elasticity implies that current price changes in no way affect a person's expectations concerning future prices. If the elasticity is unity, "a change in current prices will change expected prices in the same direction and in the same proportion."

[10] League of Nations, *International Currency Experience.* A partial reappraisal of this kind has recently been performed in S. C. Tsiang's "Fluctuating Exchange Rates in Countries with Relatively Stable Economies: Some European Experiences after World War I," *Int. Mon. Fund Staff Papers,* 7 (October, 1959), 244–73.

[11] Friedman has expressed the same opinion in his *Essays,* p. 176, n. 9.

[12] J. R. Hicks, *Value and Capital* (2d ed.; London: Oxford University Press, 1946), esp. chaps. xx–xxii.

[13] *Ibid.,* p. 205.

Under elastic expectations, "a change in current prices makes people feel that they can recognize a trend."[14]

In the later chapters, Hicks investigates the implications of elasticities of expectations for dynamic stability:

If elasticities of expectations are generally greater than unity, so that people interpret a change in prices, not merely as an indication that the new prices will go on, but as an indication that they will go on changing in the same direction, then a rise in all prices by so much *per cent.* (with constant rate of interest) will make demands generally greater than supplies, so that the rise in prices will continue. A system with elasticities of expectations greater than unity, and constant rate of interest is definitely unstable.[15]

A too literal interpretation of this and other passages would make expected prices primarily a function of current prices and current price changes. This clearly overstates the importance of the latter for people's expectations. At worst, it reverses the most plausible chain of cause and effect. The level of current prices is, of course, an important guide for an individual's appraisal of future prices. But current price *changes* should, in general, only have a relatively tenuous effect on the behavior of rational speculators unless foresight is extremely imperfect.[16] The reverse causation, on the other hand, may reasonably be expected to be significant. Once people have made up their minds what future prices are likely to be (more or less independently, in my view, of any price changes at the instant they form their opinion), they may very well undertake steps to use the differential between current and expected prices to their best advantage. The volume of their spot purchases or sales, and hence the movement of current prices, among other things, will depend primarily on the magnitude of that differential.

Let us assume, for the sake of argument, that current price changes are indeed an important signal determining people's expectations. If these expectations are elastic and speculators tend to consider a price increase at a given instant as an indication that future prices are likely to rise even more, the resulting spot purchases can be called "destabilizing" only when the speculators are

[14] *Ibid.*

[15] *Ibid.*, p. 255.

[16] This view is also taken in S. C. Tsiang's "A Theory of Foreign-Exchange Speculation under a Floating Exchange System," *Journal of Political Economy,* **66** (October, 1958), 399–418, esp. 404–5.

overoptimistic. If their foresight was correct, the rise in the current price that would normally follow is a *stabilizing* factor. On the other hand, any force that tends to hold the current price at the old level at a time when a trend toward a permanent increase in the future equilibrium price is already clearly discernible is *destabilizing*. For it must necessarily prevent a movement to the new equilibrium level, the only one that matters, when it keeps the rate to the old. Only human inertia may continue to see the latter as the equilibrium level because it has become accustomed to it. It can happen and has indeed happened repeatedly in recent history that the process is self-accelerating under a sleepy monetary policy. Whatever disturbances may then result are most appropriately imputed to the monetary authority, and it must be identified as the true destabilizer.[17]

Among modern writers, Milton Friedman has identified himself most clearly with the view that speculation must be stabilizing if it is to be profitable for speculators as a group:

People who argue that speculation is generally destabilizing seldom realize that this is largely equivalent to saying that speculators lose money, since speculation can be destabilizing in general only if speculators on the average sell when the currency is low in price and buy when it is high.[18]

He is cautious enough to add, however:

It does not, of course, follow that speculation is not destabilizing; professional speculators might on the average make money while a changing body of amateurs regularly lost larger sums. But, while this may happen, it is hard to see why there is any presumption that it will; the presumption is rather the opposite.[19]

And in a footnote he continues:

A warning is perhaps in order that this is a simplified generalization of a complex problem. A full analysis encounters difficulties in separating "speculative" from other transactions, defining precisely and satisfactorily "destabilizing speculation," and taking account of the effects of

[17] See *ibid.*, pp. 412–13. For an empirical example, see the description of French monetary policy in Tsiang's more recent article, "Fluctuating Exchange Rates in Countries with Relatively Stable Economies," *Int. Mon. Fund Staff Papers,* 7 (October, 1959), esp. 259–73.

[18] *Essays*, p. 175.

[19] *Ibid.*

the mere existence of a system of flexible rates as contrasted with the effects of actual speculative transactions under such a system.[20]

Similar views have been voiced by A. P. Lerner[21] and F. A. Lutz.[22] In his major work on international trade, J. E. Meade leans toward the belief that speculation will usually be stabilizing.[23]

Probably the earliest precise statement of the position that de-stabilizing speculation must be unprofitable for the body of speculators as a whole is due to John Stuart Mill:

For it often happens that speculative purchases are made in the expectation of some increase of demand, or deficiency of supply, which after all does not occur, or not to the extent which the speculator expected. In that case the speculation, instead of moderating fluctuations, has caused a fluctuation of price which otherwise would not have happened, or aggravated one which would. But in that case the speculation is a losing one, to the speculators collectively, however much some individuals may gain by it. . . . The operations, therefore, of speculative dealers, are useful to the public whenever profitable to themselves; and though they are sometimes injurious to the public, by heightening the fluctuations which their more usual office is to alleviate, yet whenever this happens the speculators are the greatest losers.[24]

W. J. Baumol has attempted to provide specific examples to show that this is not universally true.[25] Baumolian speculators are what might be called "piggy-back operators": they take a rise in the price as an indication that it will rise still further, and their speculative purchases at such a time produce exactly this result. They reverse themselves before the price path in the absence of all speculation would have reached its peak, and so initiate a cumulative downward movement. If the non-speculative market is characterized by a sinusoidal price path, Baumol's speculators again produce a sinusoidal cycle, but one of shorter duration, and hence with increased frequency of oscillation. The amplitude of fluctua-

[20] *Ibid.*

[21] *The Economics of Control* (New York: Macmillan, 1944), p. 70 and chap. viii.

[22] "The Case for Flexible Exchange Rates," *Banca Nazionale del Lavoro Quarterly Review*, 7, No. 31 (December, 1954), 184.

[23] *The Balance of Payments*, chap. xviii.

[24] *Principles of Political Economy*, Book IV, chap. ii, sec. 5.

[25] "Speculation, Profitability, and Stability," *Review of Economics and Statistics*, 39 (August, 1957), 263–71.

tion may (not necessarily must) be larger than that in the absence of speculation while the piggy-back operators may nevertheless, as a body, earn positive "profits." Baumol shows that, in addition, their activities may cause an explosion of an otherwise damped price oscillation.

This does not affect the conclusions we derived in the previous section, however. Whereas positive "profits" (according to Baumol's somewhat ambiguous definition of profits; see n. 4 above) may not be a sufficient condition for "piggy-back speculation" to be stabilizing,[26] profit-*maximization* necessarily is. Baumol's results suggest themselves naturally. Whereas the solution of the variational problem of maximizing an integral such as (3) in section 1 of this chapter will in general only yield one profit-maximizing function $\hat{s}(t)$, and one that will with certainty lower the amplitude of fluctuation, there is an infinity of other functions $s(t)$ that also guarantee positive, though lower, profits. Among them, there may well be modes of behavior, of which Baumol presents a few special examples, that have destabilizing effects according to certain criteria of stability.

Another important subgroup of functions $s(t)$ yielding nonnegative profits for the whole body of speculators is the one provided by *perfectly competitive* speculation with perfect foresight under varying degrees of freedom of entry. All of them act in a stabilizing way, as section 1 has shown. It is easily realized that Baumol's speculators cannot possibly be maximizing profits and at the same time have even approximately accurate foresight. In all his examples, the market is left with trendless sinusoidal fluctuations, a field day for a supplementary field of "super"-speculators who, in their turn, would flatten out the oscillations which the activities of the previous, non-profit-maximizing operators have left over. It will be observed that, in Hicks's language, Baumol's models are characterized by high elasticity of expectations. The possibility of destabilizing movements arises primarily from the assumption that changes in current prices may exercise a strong in-

[26] Telser concludes that they are a sufficient condition ("A Theory of Speculation Relating Profitability and Stability," p. 299). This does not contradict Baumol's conclusions since the models of the two authors differ essentially. Telser, unlike Baumol, makes the activities of non-speculators depend *only* on the price and not on its rate of change, a procedure that appears to me to be the only legitimate one.

fluence on people's price expectations.[27] Another cogent objection to Baumol's analysis is, as has been stressed earlier, that part of the speculative profits in his models is illusory, since accumulation of inventories over a cycle is not precluded, as it should be. Furthermore, even the supposedly "non-speculative" group in Baumol's models reacts to *changes* in prices as well as to the actual price level. Such behavior is essentially speculative. His "speculative" group can therefore legitimately be said to include only part of all speculators, a fact which precludes an unambiguous appraisal of the influence of speculation as such on the basis of his models.[28]

The presumption of high elasticity of expectations is less justified the more nearly correct speculators' expectations are. If they foresaw future price movements with perfect accuracy, only the level of current and expected future prices would influence their actions, never their rate of change. On the other hand, dependence of expectations on the current rate of change of an exchange rate is increasingly likely the more uncertain its future path. Some continuity and predictability of exchange-rate movements is therefore an indispensable prerequisite if speculation should adequately perform its economic function. Herein lies the undeniable kernel of truth in the arguments of protagonists of pegged rates.

It has been my experience that the presentation of a theory of speculation based on our assumptions usually encounters strong opposition. To no small extent, this is probably attributable to a deep-rooted association of speculation with disturbance and disequilibrium. Among more concrete objections, one of the more persuasive ones is the contention that the interaction of speculators' expectations is likely to generate its own momentum and may lead to violent convulsions of the time path of an exchange rate even when foresight concerning the behavior of non-speculators is highly accurate. Purely theoretical considerations cannot hope to refute this objection. Only empirical evidence can tell whether the actual behavior of exchange speculators belies the conclusions suggested by a model that neglects interaction of speculative expectations. The

[27] The amplitude of Baumol's price path (11), e.g., is increased faster (or damped less) the greater is the dependence of speculators' excess demand (9) on the first time derivative of the price path. "Speculation, Profitability, and Stability," p. 268.

[28] See Telser, "A Theory of Speculation Relating Profitability and Stability," and Baumol's "Reply," *Review of Economics and Statistics*, Vol. 41 (1959).

consensus nowadays seems to be that most of the available evidence does. Nurkse's League of Nations study is usually cited to support this claim.[29] It should not be too surprising that speculators' anticipations should often have turned out to be incorrect under the chaotic conditions of the depression years when even policymakers frequently had no idea what to do next. Concerning that other period of lively exchange-rate fluctuation, the years following World War I, today's widely accepted views are contradicted by the testimony of a contemporary observer who could boast of an unusually intimate acquaintance with the practical aspects of currency speculation. This was Keynes's appraisal:

We may safely attribute most of the major fluctuations of the exchanges from month to month to the actual pressure of trade remittances, and not to speculation. . . . General opinion greatly overestimates the influence of exchange speculators acting under the stimulus of merely political and sentimental considerations. Except for brief periods the influence of the speculator is washed out; and political events can only exert a lasting influence on the exchanges in so far as they modify the internal price level, the volume of trade, or the ability of a country to borrow on foreign markets.[30]

The wide fluctuations in the leading exchanges over the past three years [i.e., 1921–24] . . . have been due, not to the presence of speculation, but to the absence of a sufficient volume of it relative to the volume of trade.[31]

The reluctance of the Central Banks to operate on the forward market may be partly due to their habitual exaggeration (sometimes in search of an alibi for responsibility) of the influence of speculation.[32]

Speculators were a more active element in the market for French francs from 1924 to 1926. Whether their activities were "destabilizing" then is debatable. S. C. Tsiang's recent article concludes that the French experience does not lend itself to this interpretation, as the folklore of economics would have us believe.[33] As Tsiang points out, no other outcome but perennial inflation could possibly

[29] *International Currency Experience* (New York: Columbia University Press, 1944), chap. v.

[30] *Monetary Reform* (New York: Harcourt, Brace, 1924), pp. 122–23.

[31] *Ibid.*, p. 148.

[32] "The Future of the Foreign Exchanges," *Lloyds Bank Monthly Review*, October, 1935, p. 531.

[33] "Fluctuating Exchange Rates in Countries with Relatively Stable Economies."

be expected from the French policy during these years of having the central bank peg interest rates and supply the public with any desired amount of credit at these rates.[34]

Our theoretical conclusions receive even stronger support from the most important experiment with flexible exchange rates after the Second World War. The amplitude of oscillation of the Canadian dollar since 1950 can be considered minimal by any standards, in spite (or *because?*) of its exposure to all imaginable speculative forces and the almost complete withdrawal of the Canadian authorities from the exchange markets. The maximum amplitude of fluctuation of the Canadian dollar since 1952 has been below 5 per cent. The behavior of speculators in Canadian dollars has been analyzed in detail by R. R. Rhomberg.[35] He concludes that the available evidence lends strong support to the hypothesis that speculators have, on the whole, acted in a stabilizing manner. Similar conclusions are drawn by S. C. Tsiang from the Peruvian experience with flexible rates.[36] Another case that seems to provide persuasive evidence in favor of our contention is that of Lebanon, where freely fluctuating exchange rates have *de facto* been in effect since 1949. A detailed study of this experiment would be a rewarding task.

All the instability typically associated with oligopoly can be anticipated in a speculative market of oligopolistic structure. Currency markets, however, approach the ideal of a perfectly competitive market about as closely as can ever be expected in the real world. Unless prevented by exchange controls or voluntary restrictions on foreign-exchange speculation by banks and dealers in re-

[34] *Ibid.*, pp. 271–73. Pierre Mendès-France's doctoral thesis also makes interesting reading in this connection. *Le redressement financier français en 1926 et 1927* (Paris: Librairie générale de droit et de jurisprudence, 1928).

[35] "Fluctuating Exchange Rates in Canada: Short-Term Capital Movements and Domestic Stability," Ph.D. diss., Yale University, 1959. Summarized in "Canada's Foreign Exchange Market," *Int. Mon. Fund Staff Papers*, 7 (1960), 439–56. A different opinion is expressed in H. C. Eastman's "Aspects of Speculation in the Canadian Market for Foreign Exchange," *Canadian Journal of Economics and Political Science*, 24 (1958), 355–72.

[36] "An Experiment with a Flexible Exchange Rate System: The Case of Peru, 1950–54," *Int. Mon. Fund Staff Papers*, 5 (1957), 449–76. The Peruvian system he describes is not, however, that of a freely fluctuating exchange rate in the strict sense of the term. Two free rates existed simultaneously and foreign-exchange transactions were subjected to certain controls.

sponse to "moral suasion," everybody with money in the bank or under his mattresses is a potential currency speculator, and those without can borrow some. The possibility of speculative forward operations on narrow margins provides speculators with added leverage.

The view that speculation will normally be stabilizing has here been put forward as the most plausible hypothesis, but by no means as an inevitable necessity. Exchange-rate flexibility provides economic policy with an additional and badly needed degree of freedom, but does not deprive policymakers of any of the traditional tools. The case for fluctuating rates should not be misunderstood to stand or fall on the hypothesis that speculation will always be stabilizing. Whenever this hypothesis should turn out to be wrong, as it occasionally might, the authorities have at their disposal all the traditional means of correcting excesses and are free to use them as they see fit. The following chapter will stress the relatively effortless means of stabilizing exchange rates through intervention on forward markets, a highly promising device which has hardly ever been used, in spite of its many attractive features and its strong advocacy by Keynes and others.

# 3

## CURRENCY SPECULATION UNDER THE GOLD STANDARD

From the time of David Hume up to the 1930's, economists saw the changes in the price level which were supposed to follow movements of gold between countries as the principal force that tended to re-establish equilibrium after any disturbance in a country's balance of payments.[37] The willingness of central banks in different countries to buy and sell gold at a fixed price in terms of their own currencies established a gold parity for every currency. Their ratios provided mint parities between the currencies concerned, around which the actual market rates tended to fluctuate within the narrow

---

[37] Chap. ii, sec. 4 has shown that the classical explanation, taken at face value, is logically inconsistent. The present section will argue that Keynesian income effects are not, as commonly believed, an acceptable alternative explanation for the surprisingly smooth adjustment in the short run that puzzled observers, although they provide a valid interpretation of *long-run* adjustment processes in a world in which, unlike the one we live in, governments do not pursue full-employment policies.

margin determined by the spread between the buying and selling prices for gold of central banks and shipping charges between the respective banking centers.

Supply and demand for foreign exchange become perfectly elastic at the "gold points."[38] This prevents a movement of the exchange rate outside these limits. The perfect elasticity of the supply schedule at the gold-export point, for example, is due to purchases of gold by arbitrageurs from the domestic central bank for the purpose of selling it to the central bank abroad and subsequent repatriation of the proceeds. Gold arbitrageurs reap profits without incurring any risks whenever the foreign currency appreciates ever so slightly beyond the point at which the gold price differential just covers the cost of shipping and insurance. As long as banks traditionally keep, or central banks require them to keep, a certain reserve ratio of gold against their depositors' claims (or where the legal gold reserve requirement holds, one stage removed, for the central bank, together with reserve requirements in the form of deposits with the central bank for the commercial banking sector), the outflow of specie causes a reduction in the money supply. According to the quantity theory of money, a fall in the internal price level follows. Eventually, so the classical economists argued, the gold outflow is checked as commercial exports are favored and imports discouraged by the relative decline of domestic prices.[39]

Large-scale gold flows were relatively uncommon. It appeared surprising that the small changes in the relevant variables which usually occurred should account for the swift adjustments in balances of payments that could be observed. After the emergence of Keynesian income analysis, it was thought that the clue to the phenomenon had to be sought in the *income* changes induced by the trade surplus or deficit (with or without a simultaneous gold movement).[40] Given a positive marginal propensity to spend and initial

[38] Cf. F. Machlup, "The Theory of Foreign Exchanges," *Economica*, NS, Vol. 6 (1939–40); reprinted in AEA, *Readings in the Theory of International Trade* (Philadelphia: Blakiston, 1950), p. 130. See also the context of Fig. 7 in the following chapter.

[39] The preceding chapter has shown that only changes in absorption can bring about the required effect and that the associated changes in price levels are merely a by-product without an independent role in the adjustment mechanism.

[40] Cf. L. A. Metzler, "The Theory of International Trade," in *A Survey of Contemporary Economics*, Vol. 1, H. S. Ellis, ed. (Philadelphia: Blakiston, 1949), pp. 210–54. Only changes in output and employment can be properly designated

unemployment, an export surplus, for example, leads to a multiplied increase in the real national income. If the marginal propensity to import is positive, the induced rise in imports will partially compensate for the export surplus, even though prices or the exchange rate may not change at all.[41]

One objection to this explanation of the gold mechanism is that at least the income adjustment in the country experiencing the export surplus presupposes the existence of unemployment. With

as "income effects." If money income falls, e.g., while the economy continues to be fully employed, this can only be due to a fall of certain prices. A pure price effect has occurred, even though the careless use of Keynesian variables in terms of *money* may sometimes leave the impression that we are dealing with a genuine income adjustment.

[41] In a simple national income model with no government activity, no induced investment, and no foreign repercussion,

$$Y = C(Y) + I - M(Y) + X ,$$

where  $Y$  .... real national income;
$C$  .... real consumption;
$I$  .... real investment;
$M$  .... real imports;
$X$  .... real exports.

Hence

$$\frac{dY}{dX} = \frac{1}{1 - \dfrac{\partial C}{\partial Y} + \dfrac{\partial M}{\partial Y}} .$$

With imports a function of real national income,

$$\frac{dM}{dX} = \frac{\partial M}{\partial Y}\frac{dY}{dX} = \frac{\dfrac{\partial M}{\partial Y}}{1 - \dfrac{\partial C}{\partial Y} + \dfrac{\partial M}{\partial Y}} ,$$

or

$$\frac{dM}{dX} = \frac{1}{1 + \dfrac{\partial S/\partial Y}{\partial M/\partial Y}} ,$$

where $\partial S/\partial Y$ is the marginal propensity to save. It is evident that $0 < dM/dX < 1$ as long as $\partial S/\partial Y > 0$, $\partial M/\partial Y > 0$, and that the income adjustment following a balance-of-payments disturbance must be in the right direction, but incomplete, as long as the marginal propensity to save is positive. The presence of repercussions from abroad complicates the multiplier formula but does not alter the qualitative results.

literally full employment, real income cannot rise and the adjustment cannot be due to income effects, as has been pointed out above. A more serious criticism concerns the speed of adjustment with which the foreign-trade multiplier is supposed to work. It is sometimes erroneously believed that the rise in real income must always take place instantaneously while prices move, at best, only with a time lag. This view neglects the role of inventories in the real world. The initial reaction to an unexpected rise in exports, for instance, is certainly not an instantaneous spurt in the output of a country's export industries, but rather a decline in inventories. This constitutes a fall of investment by the same amount by which exports have risen, and the short-run effect on the real national income is nil. There is a possibility that production in the export industries may be stepped up before prices rise. This is by no means firmly established as an empirical reality, however, least of all in the period of relatively full employment we have witnessed since the end of World War II. Even if it were, the consumption lag and the subsequent delay before importers manage to augment *and pay* for new orders from abroad will undoubtedly make the income mechanism at least as long-run an adjustment process as the classical price-specie flow, properly amended. It is most likely to take considerably longer.

The real clue to the smooth balance-of-payments adjustment under the gold standard must be sought elsewhere. The preceding chapter has stressed the effect of changes in interest rates on real absorption out of a given real national income. This mechanism still requires a movement of gold and the ensuing monetary contraction (or expansion) and fails to explain why large-scale gold movements occurred relatively rarely. The present chapter suggests a most convincing answer: the gold standard is the perfect example for the effectiveness of stabilizing speculation. It is somewhat misleading to classify the gold standard as a monetary standard based on rigidly pegged exchange rates. However small the margin between the gold points may generally have been, it was crucially important that the market rate was freely fluctuating between these limits. The real significance of the gold points should not be seen in the fact that gold actually started to flow as soon as the exchange rate attained one of these boundary values. For the short run, it lay in the guaranty that the rate would eventually reverse itself. As long as there was sufficient evidence that governments would continue to adhere to the gold standard, speculators ran practically no risk in "gambling" on an eventual appreciation when a country's currency was hovering near its gold-export point and on an eventual depreciation when it was close to the gold-import point. Once this is realized, the facility of balance-of-payments adjustment under the gold standard is hardly surprising. In the short run, speculative capital flows alone are sufficient to account for it, without any need for either price (i.e., absorption) or income effects.[42]

In the long run, the latter are, of course, indispensable. If the long-run adjustment process is very sluggish, speculators have reason to expect that the exchange rate will stay at one of the gold points over an extended period, and are not induced to intervene immediately. This provides the only instance in which a gold flow will actually take place even when speculators are alert and adequately equipped with liquid funds. Even then, it may be prevented by changes in the interest differential between the countries concerned. Interest arbitrage in response to changes in bank rate will be taken up in chapter iv.

[42] Recognition of this fact is not a new discovery, as the current preoccupation with income effects would lead one to suspect. Taussig, e.g., appreciated the importance of speculation as an adjustment factor (cf. *International Trade* [New York: Macmillan, 1927], pp. 216–17). Gold flows are recognized as a last resort.

# IV

## Forward Exchange Markets

A "futures" or "forward" contract calls for delivery on a specified date in the future at a price agreed upon in advance.[1] Where a sufficiently large number of traders regularly conclude contracts for future delivery of foreign exchange, an organized forward market in currencies may develop. The main purpose of the forward exchange market, as of any other market of this kind, is the creation of a hedging facility for commercial traders. An exporter, for example, may expect a future payment in foreign currency whose exact value in domestic currency is unforeseeable under a regime of fluctuating exchange rates. If he is unwilling to carry the risk of exchange fluctuations, he may relieve himself of this uncertainty by a forward sale of his expected foreign-exchange proceeds at a price known in advance.

### 1

### THE SIMPLE MATHEMATICS OF INTEREST ARBITRAGE

One of the important features of the forward exchange market is the relationship between the forward discount or premium for a foreign

[1] The term "futures market" is applied to commodity markets only. Even for these, it is usually restricted to forward markets in which a high degree of standardization of contracts with respect to quantity, delivery time, and similar features is the rule. These characteristics are designed to accommodate the needs of speculators rather than of commercial hedgers. See G. Blau, "Some Aspects of the Theory of Futures Trading," *Review of Economic Studies*, 12 (1944–45), 1–30. The standard reference work on forward exchange markets is P. Einzig's *The Theory of Forward Exchange* (London: Macmillan, 1937). Since this chapter was first written, an article by S. C. Tsiang has appeared which closely parallels the exposition adopted in it. "The Theory of Forward Exchange and Effects of Government Intervention on the Forward Exchange Market," *Int. Mon. Fund Staff Papers*, 7 (April, 1959), 75–106.

currency and the short-term interest rates at home and abroad. This relation was, to my knowledge, first pointed out in Keynes's *Tract*.[2] We shall consider a two-country model. The following variables will be used (exchange rates are again defined as units of domestic currency per unit of foreign currency):

$r_0$.................spot rate of exchange at time 0.

$r_t$.................forward rate of exchange for delivery at time $t$. $t$ is expressed as a fraction of a year.

$i_d$ and $i_f$............domestic and foreign short-term rates of interest. We shall assume that interest is compounded instantaneously. For the short time periods usually involved, no significant discrepancy arises from the fact that compounding is always discontinuous in practice, and the necessary modifications in the analysis to take account of this are elementary.

$\epsilon$.................ad valorem charges for currency conversion, expressed as a percentage of the amount exchanged. The charge will be assumed to be the same in both directions.

$\delta$.................forward premium on foreign currency, expressed as per cent per annum on the basis of the spot rate of exchange.

A holder of idle funds has the choice of leaving his money at home, in which case one unit of domestic currency will, with a domestic interest rate $i_d$, grow to

$$D = e^{i_d t} \qquad (1)$$

at time $t$, where $e$ is the basis of the natural logarithms. If capital movements between countries are unrestricted, he may alternatively transfer his funds abroad. The existence of a forward market makes it possible to take advantage of a higher foreign interest rate without incurring an exchange risk. The expected holdings of foreign exchange at time $t$ can be sold at the known forward rate simultaneously with the original transfer.

The eventual proceeds of covered interest arbitrage can be calculated as follows: at time $t = 0$, the conversion of one unit of domestic currency will, with ad valorem conversion charges of $\epsilon$ per cent,

[2] J. M. Keynes, *Monetary Reform* (New York: Harcourt, Brace, 1924), chap. iii, Part IV.

yield $(1 - \epsilon)/r_0$ units of foreign exchange. Compounded at the foreign short-term interest rate $i_f$, this will grow to

$$\frac{1 - \epsilon}{r_0} e^{i_f t} \qquad (2)$$

at time $t$.

If this amount of foreign exchange has been sold forward at time $t = 0$ at the forward rate $r_t$ prevailing then, and if the movement of funds again involves transfer charges of $\epsilon$ per cent, the amount

$$F = \frac{r_t (1 - \epsilon)^2}{r_0} e^{i_f t} \qquad (3)$$

of domestic currency will be realized eventually. If

$$F \leqq D, \qquad (4)$$

all holders of idle funds in domestic currency have every reason to keep them at home. Whenever

$$F > D, \qquad (5)$$

on the other hand, they can reap entirely riskless profits (always assuming unrestricted freedom of capital movements) by transferring their funds abroad and simultaneously selling the eventual foreign-exchange proceeds forward. These transactions will tend to boost the spot and lower the forward rate; they will continue until condition (4) is restored.

Let us write out the equilibrium condition (4) in detail:

$$\frac{r_t}{r_0} (1 - \epsilon)^2 e^{i_f t} \leqq e^{i_d t}. \qquad (6)$$

Applying the same reasoning to holders of foreign-currency balances at time $t = 0$, we deduce the second equilibrium condition

$$\frac{r_0}{r_t} (1 - \epsilon)^2 e^{i_d t} \leqq e^{i_f t}. \qquad (7)$$

The combination of both conditions yields the boundaries for the relative divergence between spot and forward rates of exchange:

$$(1 - \epsilon)^2 e^{(i_d - i_f)t} \leqq \frac{r_t}{r_0} \leqq \frac{e^{(i_d - i_f)t}}{(1 - \epsilon)^2}. \qquad (8)$$

The forward rate for a foreign currency can be expressed as its

[ 67 ]

premium or discount on the spot rate, normalized as a percentage per annum of the latter, i.e.,

$$\frac{r_t}{r_0} = 1 + t\delta, \tag{9}$$

where $t$ is, as before, the life span of forward contracts, expressed as a fraction of a year. Substituting this in (8), taking logarithms of the inequalities and subtracting $t(i_d - i_f)$ from the result, we get

$$2 \log (1 - \epsilon) \leqq \log (1 + t\delta) - t (i_d - i_f) \leqq -2 \log (1 - \epsilon). \tag{10}$$

Hence,

$$|\log (1 + t\delta) - t (i_d - i_f)| \leqq 2 |\log (1 - \epsilon)|, \tag{11}$$

or, to a first-order approximation,[3]

$$| \delta - (i_d - i_f) | \leqq \frac{2 |\log (1 - \epsilon)|}{t}. \tag{12}$$

Let us first assume, as is usually done in theoretical discussions of the forward market, that transfer costs are zero. The inequality (12) then reduces to the single equilibrium equation

$$\delta = i_d - i_f. \tag{13}$$

Equation (13) expresses the familiar fact that the premium or discount (per annum) tends to equal the interest differential, the currency of the country with the *lower* interest rate being the one that exhibits a forward *premium*. If short-term interest rates in both countries are identical, spot and forward rates of exchange are forced into equality. The fulfilment of (13) requires not only the absence of all transfer charges but also perfect competition among interest arbitrageurs. Profit-maximization by a monopoly arbitrageur would, even when transfer is costless, leave one of the inequalities

$$\delta < i_d - i_f \quad \text{or} \quad \delta > i_d - i_f, \tag{14}$$

derived by reversing one or the other of the inequalities in (6) or (7). It can be either one of the two; a moment's reflection makes it clear that the profits of a monopoly arbitrageur depend on the existence of an absolute difference, irrespective of the sign of that difference. But the possibility of pure monopoly in interest arbitrage can be ruled out with practical certainty in any case.

[3] Obtained by expanding $\log (1 + t\delta)$ in its Taylor series and retaining only the linear term. Cf., e.g., R. G. D. Allen, *Mathematical Analysis for Economists* (London: Macmillan, 1938), p. 456.

When there are transfer costs ($\epsilon > 0$), we see from condition (12) that, with a given interest differential, the forward premium or discount has some leeway to vary between certain limits. In addition, the length of the time period over which the forward contract extends becomes a factor determining the limits of variability. The link between spot and forward rates brought about by interest arbitrage is the more tenuous the shorter is the term of the forward contracts on the market in question. On the other hand, the link provided by speculation will then be all the stronger.

Bank and brokerage charges on capital movements between countries are usually insignificant, at least for large transactions. It has nevertheless usually been observed that covered interest arbitrage will only be induced when the spread between forward premium and short-term interest differential exceeds $\frac{1}{2}$ per cent per annum.[4] Relation (12) is also important as an explanation of the large divergence between forward premium and interest differential that can often be observed when exchange controls are in effect. The difficulty of private capital transfer in the presence of exchange controls can be interpreted as an increase of $\epsilon$. Some devious ways of moving funds usually remain even under the strictest controls, although the costs of transfer may become quite prohibitive. Relation (12) gives an indication of the sharply progressive spreading of the limits of variability between spot and forward rates as the costs of transfer increase.

Experience has shown that even at times when no artificial barriers to capital movements existed and both spot and forward rates were fluctuating freely, covered interest arbitrage has frequently failed to occur on a large enough scale to narrow the gap between forward premium and interest differential to the level indicated by transfer costs. The *only* possible explanation for this phenomenon is absence of a sufficient volume of liquid funds for the purpose of covered interest arbitrage.[5] In particular, excessive speculation or a lopsided exchange market on account of a sudden imbalance in the current account are by themselves *not* sufficient to explain a persistent divergence. As soon as speculative short sales of a currency drive it to a forward discount exceeding the margin

[4] This was already pointed out by Keynes in *Monetary Reform*, p. 128.

[5] This factor was acknowledged by Keynes (*Monetary Reform*, pp. 140–41) and has been stressed particularly by R. G. Hawtrey in *The Art of Central Banking* (London: Longmans, Green, 1932), pp. 406–11.

indicated by transfer charges, covered interest arbitrage immediately becomes profitable and, given a sufficient volume of arbitrage funds, tends to reduce that discount. Incautious intuition might lead one to believe that interest arbitrageurs would not be likely to undertake forward purchases of a currency that is under speculative attack. The flaw in this objection is revealed when it is realized that the only possible type of behavior of holders of liquid funds that would *fail* to reduce the forward discount created by bear speculation is to leave these funds at home. This alternative is, however, always less profitable than covered interest arbitrage, irrespective of whether or not speculators' expectations turn out to be correct. Another alternative, speculative spot sales of home currency without forward purchases (a type of transaction whose immediate effects are indistinguishable from uncovered interest arbitrage), again tends to reduce the forward discount. Any spot sales, whether or not they are accompanied by forward transactions, presuppose the availability of liquid funds, of course.

Of the factors that may limit the intervention of a sufficient volume of liquid funds in interest arbitrage, the one of least theoretical, but of obvious practical, interest is mere ignorance. The only other possibility—that the public is fully aware of the profits to be gained by arbitrage operations, but does not dispose of enough liquid funds for this purpose—is intriguing in view of the present state of monetary theory. For if true, it would suggest that the emphasis currently given to the existence of idle cash balances and the problems they supposedly create for monetary policy has been exaggerated.[6] Although it is difficult to find evidence in print, this is also an appropriate occasion to warn of the inconsistency in arguing that (*a*) shortage of liquid funds may prevent the equilibration of forward premia and interest differentials and that (*b*) fluctuating exchange rates would be highly unstable because of the movements of a large volume of volatile speculative funds between countries. The truth, it would seem, must lie somewhere in the middle. Under normal circumstances, one would expect that there should at least be no acute shortage of funds whose holders are able to take advantage of riskless interest differentials and willing to do so if the opportunity is pointed out to them. The mobilization of these funds for the purpose of countercyclical policy seems to be

[6] A. H. Hansen, *Monetary Theory and Fiscal Policy* (New York: McGraw-Hill, 1949), chap. iv.

a most promising policy tool, whose use will be analyzed in detail in the last section of this chapter.

Another complication arises from the fact that in the real world there is more than just one short-term interest rate from which the interest differential relevant for the forward premium on a currency could be unambiguously determined.[7] For all these reasons, the supply of arbitrage funds will not be infinitely elastic in practice, as postulated for the purposes of the purely theoretical treatment in this chapter.[8]

The link between spot and forward exchange rates provided by interest arbitrage has a close parallel in all commodity futures markets. As the forward price for a commodity increases relative to its spot price, a point will be reached at which "time arbitrageurs" can reap riskless profits from spot purchase, storage, and simultaneous forward sale of the commodity. Competitive arbitrageurs will bid up the spot price and lower the forward price until the differential between the two exactly equals the cost of storage and insurance. For commodities, the relationship between spot and forward prices is asymmetrical, however. A low price of futures can "pull down" the spot price only to a limited extent; it is impossible to compensate for purchases of futures by spot sales beyond the level of current inventories. No such asymmetry holds in the forward market for foreign exchange. Even though domestic interest arbitrageurs may have only a limited "inventory" of foreign currency for spot sales, foreigners will be able as well as willing to supply the required volume of spot exchange if the foreign currency is at a sufficiently large forward discount.

A final word on another aspect of interest arbitrage which Einzig has stressed.[9] We have argued that the equilibrium conditions (6) and (7) are brought about by the effect of transfers of funds on spot and forward exchange rates. Such movements will, however, also affect interest rates in the two countries, as was shown in chapter ii. The direction of change of interest rates will tend to help realize the equilibrium conditions, as is easily seen.

[7] Einzig, *The Theory of Forward Exchange,* chap. xviii.

[8] Tsiang shows how the equilibrium of the forward exchange market can be determined under the assumption of finitely elastic supply of arbitrage funds. "The Theory of Forward Exchange and Effects of Government Intervention on the Forward Exchange Market," pp. 95–99.

[9] *The Theory of Forward Exchange,* esp. chap. xxi, "The Theory of Reciprocity."

## COMMERCIAL TRADE AND THE
## FORWARD MARKET

Under the classical gold standard, changes in a country's bank rate were seen as an important supplementary tool for safeguarding exchange stability. If a currency was under pressure, a gold outflow could presumably be prevented by raising the bank rate (and with it, the whole pattern of short-term interest rates). Apart from the effects of interest-rate changes on internal spending in the long run, the higher returns on short-term investments would attract funds from abroad. As a result, spot demand for home currency could ideally be boosted sufficiently to equilibrate the balance of payments within the gold points without the necessity of large-scale gold movements.

The mechanical imitation of this practice for paper currencies during the period after World War I showed that the leverage of small changes in the bank rate to which central bankers had become accustomed under the gold standard had become considerably weaker. Keynes first advanced the proposition that the principal effect of changes in the interest rate under fluctuating exchanges was most likely not on the spot rate but on the forward rate.[10] This was stressed again by Kindleberger.[11] Section 1 above has demonstrated the familiar fact that interest arbitrage will always tend to make the spread between spot and forward rates equal to the interest differential between the two countries. But a widening of the spread after a change in bank rate in one of the countries may come about by a movement either of the spot or the forward rate, or both. Without additional information on the shape of the market schedules for both spot and forward exchange, nothing can be said about the relative effect on either.

The forward rate bears the entire burden of adjustment when the market schedules for spot exchange are not at all affected by a change in the interest differential. This is possible only if the schedules of market demand and supply of forward exchange (to be more precise, demand and supply from sources other than interest arbitrage) coincide everywhere. The attempt to undertake covered

[10] *Monetary Reform*, pp. 148–51.

[11] C. P. Kindleberger, "Speculation and Forward Exchange," *Journal of Political Economy*, **47** (1939), 163–81.

interest arbitrage must then fail to result in any actual forward transactions. The mere attempt to sell or buy nevertheless moves the forward rate far enough to produce the required spread in accordance with the given interest differential. Failure to realize any new forward transactions makes covered interest arbitrage impossible. As a consequence, no pressure is exercised on the spot rate from this direction.

The question is, therefore, whether excess supply of forward exchange can ever be expected to be perfectly inelastic. Some of the leading writers seem to believe that this would indeed always be true in the absence of willingness to speculate. An effect of changes in the discount rate on the spot rate of exchange, it is held, can occur only to the extent that uncovered interest arbitrage takes place, or where independent speculation makes additional forward transactions by covered arbitrage possible.[12]

This view overlooks the activities of those commercial traders who regularly cover in the forward market. These importers and exporters will necessarily take the level of the *forward*, not of the spot, rate of exchange as their strategic variable.

Figure 6 illustrates this.[13] $S_0$ and $D_0$ are spot supply and demand of foreign exchange from commercial sources; $S_t$ and $D_t$ indicate amounts of forward exchange supplied and demanded by commercial exporters and importers, both functions of the forward rate $r_t$ (defined as before). For the time being, we shall assume that speculation (including uncovered interest arbitrage) is entirely absent. If, to give one purely hypothetical illustration of coincidence of market schedules, both forward schedules were perfectly inelastic at the same quantity abscissa, the underlying commodity demand for imports would have to be perfectly inelastic and the demand for exports unit-elastic. This is easily seen with the aid of the tools developed in chapter i. It is obvious that such a curious coincidence is ruled out for all practical purposes. For stability in a free forward

<hr>

[12] Keynes, *Monetary Reform*, p. 150, n. 1; Kindleberger, "Speculation and Forward Exchange." In one passage, however, the latter author recognizes that regular exports and imports do impart some elasticity to the forward schedules (p. 173).

[13] This type of diagram, familiar in the demonstration of spatial price equilibrium, was first used for the analysis of intertemporal market relations by P. A. Samuelson in his "Intertemporal Price Equilibrium: A Prologue to the Theory of Speculation," *Weltwirtschaftliches Archiv*, 79 (1957), 181–219.

market, the schedules must have the usual shape in the neighborhood of the equilibrium rate, as in Figure 6.

Let us assume that, initially, there is no interest differential, so that spot and forward rates are identical.[14] A rise of the domestic bank rate will, with the usual process of covered interest arbitrage, induce an increase in spot supply of foreign exchange ($S_0'$) and a simultaneous rise in forward demand ($D_t'$) until the spread between spot and forward rate, $d = \bar{r}_t - \bar{r}_0$, reaches the level required by the given interest differential. As long as the forward market schedules display at least some elasticity, positive amounts of

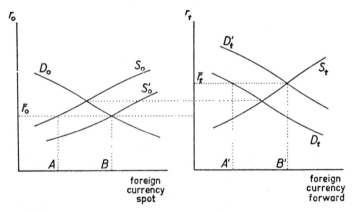

FIG. 6.—Equilibrium in the spot and forward markets of foreign exchange with interest arbitrage. Spot sales by arbitrageurs ($AB$) equal their forward purchases ($A'B'$).

foreign exchange, $AB$ and $A'B'$, will be traded in the two markets. $AB$ and $A'B'$ are equal except for the interest accrual during the time period when the funds are held in domestic banks. Inevitably, both spot and forward rates have to adjust in this case, even though speculation is assumed absent. Keynes's view is thus contradicted.

The impact on the spot rate may nevertheless be insignificant if the forward market is very thin compared to the spot market. A large price change may then occur in the former in response to a demand or supply shift small enough to cause almost no effect on the spot rate. It would appear that this condition has often been

[14] For simplicity, it has been assumed that the activities of commercial traders alone bring about equality of the two rates. We again postulate perfectly elastic supply of arbitrage funds.

fulfilled in the past. There is no very good a priori reason why it should be so, however. Thin forward markets are merely a reflection of commercial traders' ignorance, a condition that is certainly not beyond hope of correction. Under such circumstances, the really decisive factor is indeed the extent of speculative activity. Speculation will again be all the more useful the more accurate the anticipations of speculators are. In a hypothetical world in which foresight is perfect and transfer costs are zero, competitive speculation would tend to set the forward rate precisely at the level the spot exchange rate will reach at the maturity date of forward contracts. To the extent that the level of the spot rate in the future is unaffected by the rate of interest prevailing in previous periods, the impact of changes in the discount rate would then tend to fall entirely on the spot rate of exchange.

It can be convincingly argued that the forward market should be no less active than the spot market even in the absence of speculation if commercial traders are sophisticated and if, as is normally true, the functions of the participants in international trade are sufficiently specialized. Exporters or importers who negotiate contracts stipulating payment in foreign currency in three months' time will, unless they deliberately want to assume exchange risks, deal *exclusively* in the forward market. Contracts on three months' credit have traditionally been among the most widely used in foreign trade. To the extent that this group of traders avoids speculative positions in foreign exchange, the shapes of the forward market schedules will be largely determined by the elasticities of current demand and supply of the commodities in which it trades. In Tsiang's treatment, in fact, the simplifying assumption is made that *all* commercial traders deal only on the forward market of ninety days' maturity.[15] That is, of course, not intended to be an entirely realistic assumption either. In a closely interconnected system of world trade, swift international arbitrage between the leading commodity and stock exchanges, for example, should be an important source of commercial dealings in spot foreign exchange. Other traders, again, will find it convenient to use forward markets for six, nine, or twelve months or any other maturity for which contracts are available. Although theoretical discussions, including the present one, are usually restricted to one spot and one forward

[15] "Theory of Forward Exchange and Effects of Government Intervention on the Forward Exchange Market," p. 93.

market in the interest of simplicity, the extension to any number of forward markets only increases the number of variables without introducing any new problems. To the extent that commercial demands and supplies plus speculation in any one of these markets are not equilibrated at an exchange rate in accord with the appropriate interest differential, covered interest arbitrage will step in and serve to "smooth out the edges."

The Keynes-Kindleberger view that bank rate adjustments under fluctuating exchange rates cannot, or can only rarely, be expected to induce international capital movements also conflicts with the empirical observation that forward premia have frequently diverged from the interest differentials by a wide margin. This shows beyond any doubt that forward markets lead an independent life of their own and that the adjustment of forward premia to the given interest-rate structure does not come about through automatic and instantaneous changes in bankers' and brokers' quotations, but generally requires capital movements of sufficient magnitude.[16]

3

## THE FORWARD MARKET UNDER THE GOLD STANDARD

The classical gold standard may again serve as an example of a system with a very small margin of error of speculators' foresight. For both the spot and forward rates, the gold points ($G_x$ and $G_m$ in Fig. 7) provide definite limits of variability. Once the forward rate reaches the gold export point, speculative short sales of foreign exchange will tend to make the supply of forward exchange perfectly elastic ($\bar{S}_t$ in Fig. 7), for speculators are assured that they will be able to cover themselves at this rate or less when their contracts mature (barring a change in the country's gold parity). It is obvious in this case that it cannot be actual gold flows, but only stabilizing speculation that brings about perfect elasticity at the gold points of the forward-market schedules, a fact which is easily overlooked in discussions of the spot market.

It is immediately apparent that the spot rate must be extremely sensitive to small discount-rate changes under such a system. Spot

[16] This is also emphasized by Einzig, *The Theory of Forward Exchange*, chap. xix, esp. pp. 170–71.

rate movements bump against a rigid barrier, however, once the forward premium or discount called for by the existing interest differential reaches the maximum spread permitted by the gold points. If the forward rate stands at the gold export point ($G_x$ in Fig. 7), for example, interest arbitrage cannot drive the spot rate below the gold import point.

It is instructive to investigate what happens when the monetary authority nevertheless insists on keeping the interest-rate differential at a slightly higher level than the maximum spread indicated by the gold points. Three different groups of arbitrage specialists are able to reap riskless profits in this case (Fig. 7):

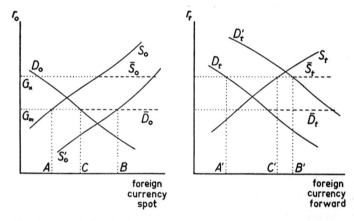

Fig. 7.—Equilibrium in the spot and forward markets of foreign exchange under the gold standard. Spot sales by interest arbitrageurs ($AB$) are absorbed in part by commercial traders ($AC$), in part by importers of gold ($CB$). Purchases of forward exchange by interest arbitrageurs ($A'B'$) are partly supplied by commercial traders ($A'C'$), partly by forward "speculators" ($C'B'$).

*a*) Let us assume that interest arbitrage produces the new schedules $S_0'$ and $D_t'$ of spot supply and forward demand for foreign exchange. Arbitrageurs sell an amount $AB$ of spot and buy $A'B'$ of forward exchange under these circumstances (equal except for interest accruals). It will be realized that we abandon our previous simplifying assumption that the supply of arbitrage funds is infinitely elastic.

*b*) With commercial traders' market schedules $D_0$, $S_0$, $D_t$, $S_t$, as before, the amount $A'C'$ of the forward purchases of interest

[ 77 ]

arbitrageurs is provided by exporters. The remainder, $C'B'$, will be sold short by foreign-exchange "speculators."[17]

c) Of the spot sales $AB$ by interest arbitrageurs, the amount $AC$ is absorbed by commercial traders while $CB$ is purchased by gold arbitrageurs for imports of gold. By keeping the interest differential at a level just slightly higher than the limits set by the gold points, the monetary authority could theoretically sustain the gold inflow indefinitely. The gold standard itself provides a check to this process. Unless gold flows are sterilized, they cause an expansion of credit at home and a contraction abroad. Even though the domestic monetary authority may retain its high nominal discount rate, other factors tend to restore equilibrium. Domestic interest rates, except for the central bank discount rate which remains fixed by assumption, will decline. The rise in interest rates abroad in the wake of monetary contraction there will reduce the interest differential, and foreign incomes and prices will tend to fall as a result of the monetary adjustment. Excess demand for spot foreign exchange from commercial sources will increase and reduce the gold inflow somewhat.

This is but one example of the rigidities imposed by the gold standard. Although the balance of payments is very sensitive to minor changes in the rate of interest, such sensitivity may not be the major objective of monetary policy. If the main purpose, for whatever reason, were a reduction of domestic income and prices, a deflationary monetary policy would inevitably become self-defeating. An attempt to raise interest rates beyond the limit imposed by the gold points will run at cross-purposes with the expansionary effect of the gold inflow induced by the increase in the domestic discount rate itself.

The reverse phenomenon has achieved greater notoriety in the history of the gold standard. If the monetary authority wants to combat a depression by easing credit, a fall in short-term interest

---

[17] Quotation marks are appropriate because, as long as the existing gold parity is not in doubt, this kind of "speculation" does not involve the slightest risk. Speculators may, of course, take a more optimistic view of the future value of domestic currency and may undertake truly speculative short sales at a forward rate *below* the gold export point. It is not necessarily true, furthermore, that the operations described here are undertaken by different people. "Pure" interest arbitrage and forward arbitrage coincide when a person undertakes uncovered interest arbitrage.

rates by more than a very limited amount is bound to be ineffectual owing to the compensating effects of the gold outflow produced by interest arbitrage. A determined antidepression policy in a single country must create the impression that the fall in the value of its currency to the gold export point is not merely a temporary matter. Speculation can therefore not be expected to step in to prevent the gold outflow.

Fiscal policy runs into the same difficulty. Any attempt by a single country to pull itself out of a depression by raising its national income entails a deterioration of its balance on current account. The contractive effect of the resulting gold outflow must inevitably defeat the original aim of expansionary fiscal measures unless a fortuitous increase in the inflow of long-term capital occurs. In this way, the gold standard imposed a degree of inflexibility on economic policy that has proved unbearable. Considerations of this nature led Keynes to argue in favor of a wider spread between the gold points.[18] Even though a widening of the limits of fluctuation was certainly highly desirable, it was the rigidity of these limits themselves, wherever they might be, that should have been the real bone of contention.

As has been pointed out in chapter ii, pegged exchange rates are, from the point of view of a single country, indistinguishable from the gold standard. The serious objections to the gold standard raised above apply to *any* system that prevents a movement of exchange rates beyond narrow limits unless the mechanism of international trade and capital movements is prevented from operating by stringent exchange controls. This can hardly be emphasized strongly enough, since it does not seem to be realized very widely.

4

SPECULATION IN FORWARD MARKETS
UNDER FLEXIBLE EXCHANGE RATES

Under fluctuating exchanges, rigid boundaries for exchange-rate movements exist neither for the spot nor for the forward market.

---

[18] *Monetary Reform*, pp. 189–91; *Treatise on Money* (New York: Harcourt Brace, 1930), **2**, 325. These issues are also discussed in two recent articles by Bent Hansen, "Interest Policy and Foreign Exchange Policy" and "Interest Policy, Foreign Exchange Policy and Foreign-Exchange Control," *Skandinaviska Banken Quarterly Review*, October, 1958, pp. 114–22, and January, 1959, pp. 15–28.

As a consequence, the effectiveness of discount policy as a tool of balance-of-payments adjustment is less certain than under the gold standard. The preceding sections have made it clear that the crucial variables are the elasticities of the spot- and forward-market schedules. If the forward market is thin or if commercial traders respond only sluggishly to changes in the forward rate, the effect of changes in short-term interest rates on the spot rate may well be insignificant. Another factor of decisive importance is the degree of perfection of speculators' foresight.

It has already been pointed out above that Keynes's presumption against a marked effect of central-bank discount policy on the spot rate appears weaker than generally believed. It is easy, furthermore, to prescribe additional policy measures that could guarantee its effectiveness. The *perfect* elasticity of the market schedules at the gold points, brought about by gold movements, speculation, and forward arbitrage is necessarily absent under fluctuating exchanges. But quite apart from the role of commercial transactions, there is ample reason to believe that speculation will normally guarantee sufficiently high elasticities of both market schedules, provided the monetary authorities have not wholly abdicated. Although covered interest arbitrage results in a forward discount on the currency of the country raising its interest rate, tighter monetary policy does not cause an increased anticipation that the actual spot rate at the later date will depreciate. Even though it is currently the orthodox view that monetary policy is a relatively ineffectual tool for the control of the business cycle, the least that can be said for it is that a tightening of credit will, other things being equal, hardly lead to (or accentuate) a rise in prices and incomes in the long run. There are strong reasons to believe, therefore, that tight money will, at the very least, not lead to a currency value three months hence below the one that was expected before.

It follows that a change in monetary policy will generally tend to make the forward rate and the *expected* actual future rate move in opposite directions. The more drastic the policy change, the wider will be the anticipated spread between the two, and the greater the expected profits of speculators who take advantage of it. To avoid confusion in the reader's mind, it is perhaps not altogether superfluous to point out that the spread between forward rate and expected future rate which we are currently discussing has nothing in common with the forward premium. The latter is a relation be-

[ 80 ]

tween the spot and the forward rate and is known precisely at any moment, whereas the former concerns two exchange rates of which one can, at best, only be expressed by a probability distribution. Interest arbitrage—the operation that tends to bring the forward premium into line with the interest differential—is a riskless venture. On the other hand, a short sale of forward exchange, the kind of transaction that would tend to reduce an expected gap between the two future rates, is an act of genuine speculation, beset with uncertainty.

It can reasonably be argued, therefore, that the latter activity will be less willingly forthcoming than interest arbitrage, but it is unreasonable to believe that it should be totally lacking.[19] Although the operation involves risk, expected unit profits of short selling will, *ceteris paribus*, grow with the extent of the interest differential and should eventually attract a large enough body of speculators to guarantee sufficiently high elasticities in the forward market. The argument that we cannot count on people to take speculative risks of this kind when exchange rates are free to fluctuate is, in my experience, often advanced by economists who would also have us believe at other times that exchange-rate flexibility would usually be accompanied by wild speculative excesses.

In this way, forward speculation provides a buffer for variations in the forward rate. It is an elastic buffer, however, unlike the inflexible limits imposed by the gold standard. As the previous section should have made amply clear, such flexibility is most desirable. The verdict that speculation is the more stabilizing the better speculators are able to judge future events applies to the forward market as well. The smaller the variance of the probability distribution of expected future exchange rates, the lower will be the risk premium that has to be offered to potential forward speculators to induce them to enter the market, and the smaller will be the average divergence between forward rates and the actual spot rates realized later for the same maturity date. Continuity of economic policy can substantially enhance the accuracy of speculators' foresight. It is a fair guess that policymakers are rarely aware of these subtle, but nonetheless highly significant, benefits of monetary stability.

[19] Einzig has pointed out that forward exchange markets were much thinner in the 1930's as compared to the period 1924–26. He also stresses, however, that the principal reason was by no means widespread unwillingness to undertake speculative forward operations, but rather active official discouragement of such transactions. *The Theory of Forward Exchange*, p. 79.

We have implicitly assumed up to this point that, starting from equality of foreign and domestic interest rates, a change in the domestic discount rate will make spot and forward rates go in opposite directions. But this is not necessarily bound to happen. If the discount rate is raised at a time when stability of the exchange rate is generally expected,[20] forward speculators may well hold the view that domestic currency is likely to appreciate after a certain time lag as the result of a fall in prices and incomes in the wake of a tightening of credit. This would tempt them to sell foreign currency short. Instead of the depreciation of domestic forward currency that covered interest arbitrage would bring about, forward speculation of this kind may, if done on a sufficiently large scale, cause forward *ap*preciation. Interest arbitrage will then make domestic spot currency appreciate not only by the full extent of the newly created interest differential but by more, as a result of the simultaneous appreciation of the forward rate. Unlike the gold standard, a flexible exchange-rate system does not impose any rigid limits to such movements. In this respect, flexible exchanges provide much wider scope for monetary policy than the gold standard.

In practice, central banks tighten credit under different conditions. They usually adopt deflationary measures at a time when an inflationary trend is already clearly discernible. An increase of domestic prices and money incomes relative to the level of incomes and prices in foreign countries makes the spot rate depreciate. With it, kept in step by forward arbitrage, goes the forward rate. A rise in *nominal* interest rates may be insufficient to check this trend.[21] Domestic currency will then, *ceteris paribus*, continue to depreciate on both the spot and the forward markets. The rise in the nominal interest differential, unless it is drastic enough to reverse price expectations, will merely lead to a larger forward discount without noticeably raising the spot rate. I suspect that it was primarily this

[20] Here and elsewhere we are concerned with the theoretical effects of hypothetical policy measures, irrespective of whether or not the monetary authorities of any given country would be likely, or well advised, to undertake these measures under the assumed circumstances.

[21] The observed ineffectiveness of monetary policy in many instances during the past thirty years may be partly explained by its timidity; in times of a *nominal* rise in interest rates, the *real* rate of interest was probably declining more often than not, and vice versa. Rational consumers or entrepreneurs are inevitably concerned with the latter, not with the former. Their lack of response is hardly surprising.

factor that prompted Keynes and Kindleberger, among others, to their negative conclusions concerning discount-rate policy under a regime of flexible exchange rates.

On the basis of the theoretical considerations pursued in this chapter, it seems legitimate to reverse the steps of the argument. From the mere fact that a given change in nominal interest rates has no observable effect on a flexible spot rate, we might infer that the interest-rate adjustment has not yet reversed the change in the real rate of interest and that more drastic measures are required. Since this argument entails rather sweeping implications for the conduct of monetary policy, I hasten to add that its validity pre-supposes the existence of an active and well-organized forward market. Where ignorance is responsible for a thin market in forward exchange, the impotence of discount policy in exerting an influence on a country's exchange rate need not surprise us. The appropriate policy to be followed when the forward market is too thin can be summarized very briefly: the authorities have to undertake those actions which well-informed forward speculators and commercial traders could be expected to bring about if the markets were active and foresight sufficiently accurate. The government (or the central bank) has an incomparable advantage over private speculators: barring the interference of politicking, it can always take the necessary measures to *prove* itself to have been correct *ex post facto*.

5

MONETARY POLICY UNDER FLEXIBLE
EXCHANGE RATES

At least since the 1930's, economists have been inclined to dispute any marked effect of monetary policy on the business cycle. To a large extent, this attitude is intimately associated with post-Keynesian thinking, although there is hardly any doubt that Keynes himself was not nearly as uncompromising on this point as some of his followers of today.[22] At this juncture, we do not want to challenge current orthodoxy, however. For the purposes of this section,

[22] In the Preface to the 1949 edition of his *Banking Policy and the Price Level* (New York: Augustus M. Kelley), Sir Dennis Robertson acknowledges his debt to Keynes and records with some amusement that Keynes's criticism of the first edition was primarily "directed towards playing down the gravity of the objections which I thought I had discovered to the policy of monetary stabilization" (p. 11).

the post-Keynesian strictures can be willingly conceded. It will be shown that a system of pegged exchange rates necessarily deprives itself of an arm of monetary policy that could very well turn out to be the most powerful one. To demonstrate the point, it suffices to pick up a few of the threads developed in the preceding sections of this chapter.

Interest arbitrage after a sufficient rise in domestic interest rates induces an inflow of funds ($AB$ in Fig. 6), depressing the spot rate of exchange $r_0$ (an appreciation of domestic currency). A necessary condition is, of course—except to the extent that uncovered arbitrage occurs—a sufficiently active forward market or adequate government policies to make that market active enough. But the consequences are more far-reaching than a mere change in the exchange rate. If $D_0$ and $S_0$ in Figure 6 are, as assumed, the spot-market schedules for foreign exchange derived from the import demand functions at home and abroad, $AB$ not only indicates the amount of capital inflow, but at the same time the value (in foreign currency) of an addition to that part of the supply of domestically available commodities that is customarily imported against spot foreign exchange. This will induce a fall in prices, or reduce inflationary pressure where it existed, *without requiring any adjustment of aggregate domestic production.*

Conversely, if the interest differential, $i_d - i_f$, becomes negative after an easing of credit by the domestic central bank, interest arbitrage produces a capital outflow associated with an export surplus of those commodities that are customarily exported against spot exchange (barring sterilization of capital flows by the monetary authorities at home and abroad). Whenever a temporary lapse from full employment occurs, an easing of credit by the monetary authority will, in addition to any possible effects on purely domestic spending, bring this stimulus into play.

This is perhaps the most persuasive reason for the advocacy of flexible exchanges in this monograph and deserves to be stressed all the more since it appears that it has never received attention elsewhere. This mechanism was undoubtedly at work even under the gold standard. Within the gold points, the exchange rate was free to vary and the foreign-trade leverage of monetary policy was operative, although its force was, as stressed before, unduly and arbitrarily limited by the unyielding restraints imposed by the gold points.

There are good reasons to believe that the use of a country's foreign accounts as a tool of adjustment should usually be much less painful than the traditional mechanism through which monetary policy is supposed to work. Insufficient price flexibility in many economies makes it inevitable that the burden of any purely domestic adjustment has to be borne by real variables to a large extent. Suppressing an inflationary trend while holding the external balance constant can therefore be expected to involve some reduction in employment, at least temporarily. If, on the other hand, the policies outlined above are adopted to check inflation, the country's currency appreciates and domestic producers are exposed to an inflow of foreign commodities at reduced prices. Since it must usually be assumed that part of a country's pattern of production consists of import-competing goods, businesses in these lines have no other choice but to conform by lowering their prices to the same level. Although it is possible that some initial unemployment occurs in this case as well, its quantitative importance should be significantly less, owing to the assumption of part of the burden of adjustment by enforced price flexibility.

In conclusion, I should like to discuss a few other related points.

1. The requirement that a positive interest differential should induce a capital *in*flow is identical with the condition for a stable static equilibrium in the exchange market. It was shown in chapter i that this condition is necessarily fulfilled in a free exchange market in the neighborhood of the equilibrium point realized at any moment. The belief that the Marshall-Lerner condition could conceivably be violated in a free market would imply the corollary that covered interest arbitrage in the presence of a positive interest differential must lead to a capital *out*flow covered by forward sales of foreign exchange. In other words, funds would flow from the market with the higher interest rate to the one with the lower.

2. The objection to our general conclusions might be raised that, while the creation of a positive interest differential tends to make domestic *spot* currency appreciate and thereby induces an additional commodity inflow, it has the opposite effect on the forward rate and the commodity movements financed through forward transactions. We recall, first of all, that this is necessarily true only where an inflationary trend is anticipated, or is expected to continue. Otherwise, both spot and forward rates might conceivably appreciate. But where it is true, a tightening of credit would tend to reduce

[ 85 ]

the availability of those commodities whose traders typically resort to the forward rather than the spot market. It might be argued that this effect is likely to cancel the impact of monetary policy via the spot exchange market.

On closer inspection, the objection turns out to be invalid. It must generally be expected that delivery of commodities whose traders use the spot market for foreign exchange will precede the delivery of commodities for which traders typically cover themselves on the forward market.[23] The first impact of tighter monetary policy on the foreign balance will therefore undoubtedly be as suggested above. Matters become a little more involved when the day of reckoning approaches for the first forward contracts concluded after the increase in the discount rate. A look at Figure 6 reveals that the domestic availability of commodities for whose payment traders had covered themselves forward must have been reduced if interest arbitrage had indeed made domestic currency depreciate. This factor alone would create inflationary pressure. But interest arbitrage is a recurring game as long as the interest differential persists. At the time when the first forward contracts mature, interest arbitrage will continue to produce the same spread between spot and forward rates by spot sales and forward purchases of foreign exchange. By itself, this factor will again put downward pressure on the price level.

The combined effect of the two forces (after the first shock which is certainly deflationary) seems to remain in doubt. The uncertainty is removed, however, once potential speculators realize the profits to be made at each stage. Unless the tightening of credit did not go far enough to arrest the long-run prospect for inflation, they will notice that the actual spot price of foreign exchange turns out to be lower all the time than the forward rate that was previously quoted for the same date. It is therefore reasonable to expect that the forward rating of foreign exchange shows a declining trend over time. Interest arbitrage will tend to make the spot rate decline with the forward rate and to boost the spot capital inflow to higher and

---

[23] Commercial traders who use the spot market and those who use the forward market at any given moment must be non-competing groups. At first glance, it would appear as if a reduction of the spot rate relative to the forward rate of exchange, say, might induce many importers to shift from coverage (for a given payment date) on the forward market to coverage on the spot market, and vice versa for exporters. The interest differential to which the spread is due will, however, make any apparent advantage of such substitution illusory.

higher levels. This insures the continuation of deflationary pressure. An additional argument relevant to the present issue will be taken up in point 6 below.

3. In theory, there is no end to the process pointed out in the preceding paragraphs until the interest differential is wiped out. Interest arbitrageurs can always realize riskless profits by keeping the forward premium in line with that differential, while no real basis for a divergence between spot and forward rates exists in the absence of an inflationary or deflationary trend. As long as capital movements are free, forward speculation will, in its turn, create pressure to reduce the forward premium to the vanishing point. The result is a continuous capital inflow into the country with the, however slightly, higher interest rate. As an increasing number of potential speculators learn to profit from forward speculation, the flow will gather momentum. The importance of this mechanism for countries with a desperate need for foreign development capital is almost too obvious to be particularly stressed, were it not for the fact that many economists and policymakers do not seem to be aware of it.

4. The principal obstacle to smooth operation of the mechanism is, as has been repeatedly stressed, thin forward markets. Whether this is due to ignorance or to other causes, the remedy is obvious: the monetary authorities themselves may provide the required volume of forward activity. Simultaneously with a tightening of credit, to give an example, the central bank can undertake forward sales of foreign exchange. This keeps the depreciation of domestic currency on forward markets within limits or prevents it altogether as interest arbitrage boosts the demand for forward exchange. Such a policy can impart any desired degree of elasticity to the forward market schedules and will insure whatever effect on the spot rate the situation calls for.[24]

The reader will notice that central-bank activity in the forward market does not impose the slightest strain on its foreign exchange reserves, unlike support of the spot market which usually has been and still is so widely practiced. Superficially, it might appear as if the threat of depletion of reserves is only put off temporarily when the central bank attempts to defend its currency in this way. This view overlooks the recurrence of events as long as the interest dif-

[24] Here and elsewhere, reference to Fig. 6 should clear up any possible difficulties of interpretation.

ferential is preserved and no change in expectations has occurred. At the time when the forward contracts mature and the central bank is obliged to deliver foreign exchange *in concreto*, interest arbitrageurs will be eagerly looking for buyers and the monetary authority will encounter no difficulty in acquiring any amount of spot exchange it needs. For it is always free again to sell the required quantity of forward exchange to satisfy the needs of interest arbitrage if forward speculators should be unwilling to supply it.

It is evident that such a policy cannot be a *substitute* for monetary and fiscal restraint in a time of inflationary pressure. Over-all economic policy has to instil sufficient confidence in the long-run stability of the currency; otherwise, the forward activities of the authorities will merely amount to a subsidy to speculators who engage in a snowballing capital flight in the safe anticipation that the exchange value of the threatened currency will have to give way sooner or later.

5. The monetary authority is in a position to continue this game indefinitely without running a true exchange risk. Not only can it always make sure that it will be able to cover itself in time for its short sales of foreign exchange but also that it can do so without a loss. The rule is simple: the authorities have to hold short sales of forward exchange and/or the interest differential at a sufficiently high level to let interest arbitrage always keep the spot rate of foreign exchange at the level for which the maturing forward contracts had been concluded.

6. The central bank is free not to limit its activities to forward markets with the traditional contracts of three months or less. It may inaugurate forward markets for six-, twelve-, or eighteen-month delivery or any other time span that the needs of international trade call for. In each of them, it can apply the rules described above and insure the virtual absence of exchange risks for its own operations as well as, incidentally, for exporters and importers. The establishment of forward markets with many different maturities would answer a widespread objection to flexible exchanges; the charge that they disrupt trade because of the greater uncertainty of future exchange-rate movements. The opportunity to hedge for expected proceeds or liabilities many months or possibly several years ahead of time must immeasurably enhance the willingness to conduct foreign trade.

On closer inspection, the doubts that arose in point 2 above are seen to be a result of the assumption that only one type of forward contract is available. The inauguration of a whole gamut of forward markets with different maturities is bound to reduce the partial cancellation of the effects on business activity of a change in one rate by an opposite movement of the forward rate for the next longer maturity. If, for example, most of the compensating change were pushed onto the forward rate for eighteen-month delivery, its effect on present economic conditions would undoubtedly be insignificant.

7. In view of the fact that action in the forward market does not require official reserves of foreign exchange, there is no convincing reason why central banks or exchange stabilization funds should not confine any intervention they may want to undertake *exclusively* to the forward market. By appropriate variations of interest rates, the spot rate will be taken care of by private interest arbitrage. After this policy has been pursued for a while, there is every reason to expect that private operators will avail themselves more and more of the profitable opportunities offered by forward speculation. This would enable the monetary authorities to withdraw from intervention in the foreign-exchange markets before too long, except for an occasional demonstration that they intend to preserve long-run stability whenever the public's confidence shows signs of uncertainty.

Keynes's recommendations for intervention in the forward markets for foreign exchange became well known, but seem to have been implemented only rarely. In the *Tract*, he proposed simultaneous transactions in both spot and forward markets in order to facilitate hedging by commercial traders.[25] The central bank is supposed to avoid all exchange risks. The proposal would require the central bank to keep an additional fund of foreign exchange for this purpose. Services of this kind are currently performed by commercial banks in the major centers of international finance, and action by the central bank should only be necessary in countries whose commercial banking system is still in a rather primitive stage.

Keynes's suggestions in the *Treatise on Money* came closer to what is advocated here.[26] He there proposed management of forward exchange rates by central banks with the intention of creating a spread between the effective interest rates for domestic and foreign

[25] *Monetary Reform*, pp. 144–46.

[26] **2**, 325–27. This proposal is hinted at in one paragraph in *Monetary Reform*, p. 146.

lenders whenever this appears desirable. His principal concern was the preservation of an adequate international liquidity position without the domestic disturbances that would be provoked if monetary policy were applied to that end, rather than the deliberate use of a country's foreign balance as an instrument of domestic monetary policy.

In a number of recent articles, A. E. Jasay and J. Spraos have taken up Keynes's proposals in their criticism of the British policy of letting the forward rate fluctuate freely while the spot rate remains pegged.[27] The authors point out correctly that it was mostly non-speculative covered interest arbitrage that led to the rapid depletion of British gold and foreign-exchange reserves on several occasions in recent years. The intention to stress this aspect made them perhaps underemphasize the obvious fact that the substantial forward discount on the pound sterling which gave rise to covered arbitrage could not have occurred without a sizable volume of speculation against the pound. The remedy suggested by Jasay and Spraos is a return to the policy of pegging the forward rate. This would leave the strong inducement for speculative sales of spot currency (to the extent that this is legally possible) provided by official support of the spot rate of exchange. A more convenient and natural way of reducing the forward discount under the given circumstances would seem to be flexibility rather than pegging of *both* the spot and the forward rate.

[27] "Exchange Policy in the Forward Market," contributions by A. E. Jasay, J. Spraos, and anon., *The Banker*, Vol. 108 (April, 1958); A. E. Jasay, "Making Currency Reserves 'Go Round,'" *Journal of Political Economy*, 66 (1958), 353–56; J. Spraos, "Speculation, Arbitrage and Sterling," *Economic Journal*, 69 (1959), 1–21.

# V

## Income and Employment under Flexible Exchange Rates

National-income analysis has so far been almost entirely avoided. The application of income analysis to balance-of-payments problems has become a predominantly academic pursuit in view of the fact that the elimination of (Keynesian) unemployment is one of the arts we have finally learned to master in a satisfactory degree. In particular, governments have shown little inclination to let the vagaries of world trade interfere with full employment.

In spite of these reservations, we cannot forget that changes in an economy's foreign-trade sector do have repercussions on the level of real national income and employment which will continue to pose adjustment problems. Not only would their neglect leave a genuine gap in a study of this kind, but it would also do injustice to a significant part of the literature on flexible exchange rates.[1] For the

---

[1] The principal contributions are A. C. Harberger, "Currency Depreciation, Income and the Balance of Trade," *Journal of Political Economy*, 58 (1950), 47–60; S. Laursen and L. A. Metzler, "Flexible Exchange Rates and the Theory of Employment," *Review of Economics and Statistics*, 32 (1950), 281–99; W. F. Stolper, "The Multiplier, Flexible Exchanges, and International Equilibrium," *Quarterly Journal of Economics*, 64 (1950), 59–82; S. S. Alexander, "Effects of a Devaluation on a Trade Balance," *International Monetary Fund Staff Papers*, Vol. 2 (1951–52); J. Spraos, "Consumers' Behavior and the Conditions for Exchange Stability," and I. F. Pearce, "A Note on Mr. Spraos' Paper," both in *Economica*, N.S., 22 (1955), 137–51; H. G. Johnson, "The Transfer Problem and Exchange Stability," *Journal of Political Economy*, 64 (June, 1956), 212–25, reprinted in *International Trade and Economic Growth* (Cambridge, Mass.: Harvard University Press, 1958), chap. vii; J. Spraos, "Stability in a Closed Economy and in the Foreign-Exchange Market," *Review of Economic Studies*, 29 (1956–57), 161–76.

most part, this literature is concerned with generalizations of the Marshall-Lerner condition. Chapter i has demonstrated at some length that an equilibrium position attained by a flexible exchange rate must necessarily be statically stable. For our central topic, there is therefore little interest in further refinements of stability conditions. We shall deal exclusively with the impact of foreign trade on the level of employment under the usual assumptions underlying Keynesian analysis. Special care will be taken to make all these assumptions explicit in order to emphasize the restrictions under which the conclusions are valid.

It is well known that under pegged exchange rates and with unimpeded flow of commodities between countries—the situation characteristic of the gold standard and the conditions originally envisaged by the founders of the International Monetary Fund—business cycles are propagated with maximum impact throughout the participating countries. Flexible exchanges, disregarding all other pros and cons, act as a buffer to such disturbances.[2] Laursen and Metzler in particular have shown,[3] however, that flexible exchanges cannot serve as *perfect* stabilizers of national incomes even if it is assumed that no capital transfers[4] are permitted, so that the current account is forced into balance at every instant of time and the effect of a non-zero balance of trade on the national income is precluded.

Laursen and Metzler concentrate on the impact on aggregate demand of changes in the price level induced by movements of a flexible exchange rate. They reach the conclusion, somewhat perplexing at first, that flexible exchanges will bring about the opposite effect on output from the one experienced under pegged exchange rates: a boom in one country entails a contraction in the rest of the world. The verbal reasoning of the authors[5] that leads to this con-

[2] This fact often eludes laymen. Many people are inclined to believe that by sacrificing the perfect stability of a pegged exchange rate an additional element of instability is also imparted to output and employment.

[3] "Flexible Exchange Rates and the Theory of Employment."

[4] *Ibid.*, p. 283. To make the statement consistent, "capital transfers" have to be defined in a rather wide sense, including each and every kind of transaction that serves to finance a trade imbalance on current account, such as short- and long-term private and governmental loans, gold shipments or earmarking, changes in a country's foreign-exchange reserves, etc.

[5] *Ibid.*, pp. 284–89.

clusion is somewhat involved. The frequency with which their result has been questioned[6] indicates that it did not appear too convincing to many readers. We shall therefore attempt a restatement in simple mathematical language.

Appreciation of a country's currency, caused by a boom in the rest of the world and the subsequent increase in demand for the country's exports, will, *ceteris paribus*, lower the domestic prices of imports.[7] How does this affect the national income?

The absence of money illusion among consumers implies that real consumption $C/p$ is a function of real income $Y/p$.[8] Let money expenditure on consumer goods be expressed as a function of money income and the price level,

$$C = f(Y, p). \tag{1}$$

Absence of money illusion requires that money consumption $C$ be homogeneous of the first degree in money income and prices, i.e.,

$$\lambda C = f(\lambda Y, \lambda p) \tag{2}$$

for any positive constant $\lambda$. Equation (2) expresses the familiar condition that a doubling, for example, of all prices and money in-

---

[6] Spraos, "Consumers' Behavior and the Conditions for Exchange Stability"; Pearce, "Note"; W. H. White, "The Employment-Insulating Advantages of Flexible Exchanges: A Comment on Professors Laursen and Metzler," *Review of Economics and Statistics*, 36 (1954), 225–28.

[7] The *ceteris paribus* clause is important. In particular, changes in existing tariffs or other trade restrictions are ruled out. Otherwise, nothing definite can be said about the price changes that can be expected (see chap. vi below). We shall also adopt the Keynesian assumption of constancy or near-constancy of money prices of domestic output.

[8] $C$ . . . . . . . money expenditure on consumption.
$Y$ . . . . . . . money national income.
$p$ . . . . . . . . index of the price level. We follow the admittedly forced assumption that arguments of this type in terms of an aggregate price level are permissible. The existence even of only two goods whose prices do not move in the same proportion raises an index-number problem. But since only directions of change matter here, our qualitative conclusions will not be seriously affected by this difficulty.

Investment is assumed to be an autonomous variable. If induced investment is present, "consumption" has to be replaced by "aggregate spending," the "marginal propensity to consume" by the "marginal propensity to spend"; the analysis is otherwise unchanged.

comes will double money expenditure on consumption. Euler's theorem on homogeneous functions[9] is then applicable:

$$C = \frac{\partial C}{\partial Y} Y + \frac{\partial C}{\partial p} p \, . \tag{3}$$

Transposing terms,

$$\frac{\partial C}{\partial p} = \frac{Y\left(\dfrac{C}{Y} - \dfrac{\partial C}{\partial Y}\right)}{p} \, , \tag{4}$$

from which follows

$$\frac{\partial C}{\partial p} > 0 \, , \tag{5}$$

provided that

$$\frac{C}{Y} > \frac{\partial C}{\partial Y} \, . \tag{6}$$

Condition (6) is assured by the customary properties of the consumption function.[10] A fall in the price level will therefore lead to a decrease of expenditure on consumption.

It is easily shown that the sequence of events sketched above results in a change of real consumption in the opposite direction. To demonstrate this, we require the sign of

$$\frac{\partial \left(\dfrac{C}{p}\right)}{\partial p} = \frac{p \dfrac{\partial C}{\partial p} - C}{p^2} \, . \tag{7}$$

Substituting for $\partial C / \partial p$ from (4), we obtain

$$\frac{\partial \left(\dfrac{C}{p}\right)}{\partial p} = -\frac{Y}{p^2} \frac{\partial C}{\partial Y} < 0 \, . \tag{8}$$

The sign is unambiguously established as negative. This outcome could also be expressed by saying that the demand for consumer goods in the Keynesian framework is price-inelastic. The same is true of its income-elasticity.[11]

[9] Cf. R. G. D. Allen, *Mathematical Analysis for Economists* (London: Macmillan, 1938), p. 317.

[10] We are here concerned with short-run effects and therefore neglect qualifications à la Duesenberry, Modigliani, or Friedman.

[11] In fact, it is easily shown that price- and income-elasticity are equal in absolute value and of opposite sign. This will not surprise anyone who is familiar with the properties of homogeneous functions. Cf. P. A. Samuelson, *Foundations of Economic Analysis* (Cambridge, Mass.: Harvard University Press, 1947), p. 105.

In the absence of counteracting forces from the foreign-trade sector, the rise in (real) effective demand occasioned by a fall of import prices would boost the country's real national product. So far, we seem to be led to the conclusion that a foreign boom will, in the first instance, tend to cause a domestic expansion under flexible exchanges and in the absence of capital movements, as it would with pegged exchange rates. The next step will be to show that there are counteracting forces, although it is difficult to tell immediately whether they are strong enough to overcompensate for the real-income effect of appreciation.

In the accepted Keynesian framework, money wages and prices within a country are assumed constant (or almost constant) as long as there is unemployment and excess capacity. Under a system of *pegged* exchange rates, the values of imports and exports are then exactly proportional to their physical volumes. The traditional conclusion necessarily follows that foreign trade has no effect on the national income as long as the balance of trade is zero. But when exchange rates, and hence the terms of trade, between two countries are flexible, this is no longer true. If the *values* of exports and imports are forced into equality while their exchange ratio is altered, their physical volumes cannot have changed in the same proportion. They may, in fact, not even change in the same *direction*. A movement of the exchange rate, therefore, cannot fail to exert a direct influence on the size of the real national product, quite apart from the effect of changes in the terms of trade on domestic expenditure which we discussed above. We may safely exclude Giffen's paradox from international trade. It will now be shown that the direct foreign-trade effect of appreciation of a country's currency as the demand for its exports increases must be depressive as long as domestic prices of each country's own output remain constant.[12] The following symbols will be used:

[12] I shall continue to follow the assumption that domestic prices of domestic production do not change, not because it is very realistic, but because it provides a basis from which definite conclusions can be easily derived without too intricate a maze of mathematical derivation. The assumption is made in most of the relevant literature, including the Laursen-Metzler paper discussed here ("Flexible Exchange Rates and the Theory of Employment," *op. cit.*, p. 292). By implication, less than full employment is postulated. Our qualitative conclusions are unchanged even if domestic prices of exports should rise after foreign demand for them increases, as long as they rise by a smaller proportion than the currency appreciates. This is assured unless export supply is very inelastic.

$M$ . . . . . . . . . physical quantity of imports;

$X$ . . . . . . . . . physical quantity of exports;

$r$ . . . . . . . . . . exchange rate, defined as units of domestic currency per unit of foreign currency;

$\epsilon$ . . . . . . . . . . absolute value of the domestic elasticity of demand for imports.[13]

It simplifies matters considerably to suppose that each country exports only one homogeneous commodity. The definition of a commodity unit is entirely arbitrary for our purposes. For convenience, the units will be chosen in such a way that the domestic price of each country's exports becomes unity. Under these assumptions, the domestic price of imports equals the value of the exchange rate, $r$, and the revenue from exports in terms of home currency is equal to their physical volume. The enforcement of continuous equality between the values of exports and imports is expressed by the condition

$$X \equiv M \cdot r . \tag{9}$$

An increase in foreign demand for the country's exports will, if the previous equilibrium was stable (as it must have been if there is a free currency market with a flexible exchange rate), cause appreciation of the currency of the country we consider (a fall of $r$ under our definition). The exchange rate remains unchanged only in the limiting case when the domestic demand elasticity for imports is infinite. All consequences of a rise in the demand for exports can therefore be investigated by asking what happens as the currency appreciates while the values of imports and exports remain in balance, as stipulated.

The effect on real national income will depend on the changes in the physical volume of exports and imports. Differentiating $M$ and $X$ with respect to $r$, using (9), we obtain

$$\frac{dM}{dr} = -\frac{\epsilon \cdot M}{r} , \tag{10}$$

and

$$\frac{dX}{dr} = M + \frac{dM}{dr} \cdot r = M (1 - \epsilon) . \tag{11}$$

---

[13] This will again be a "total" elasticity in the sense of chapter i. No use is therefore made of "marginal propensities to import." This is one of the differences between our approach and that of Laursen and Metzler. See also the remarks at the end of chapter ii.

[ 96 ]

We now define a ratio

$$\frac{dX/dr}{dM/dr} = r\left(1 - \frac{1}{\epsilon}\right). \tag{12}$$

If we redefine the unit of foreign currency (and hence, once more, the physical unit of imports) so as to make $r = 1$ in the initial equilibrium, the price per unit both of exports and of imports in terms of home currency equals 1, and changes in the volumes of exports and imports by the same absolute amount have effects of equal magnitude, but of opposite sign, on real national product and employment. The ratio (12) is simplified to

$$R = 1 - \frac{1}{\epsilon}. \tag{13}$$

In the absence of Giffen's paradox, the denominator of (12) is always negative. A positive value for $R$ therefore indicates that the volume of exports will rise after an increase in foreign demand. It is easily seen that the export volume can never rise by more than that of imports (always under the assumption that Giffen's paradox does not arise). The most favorable case occurs when the domestic elasticity of import demand is infinite. Not only the foreign-trade effect, but also the real-income effect on internal consumption is then absent, since all domestic prices remain unchanged. An increase in foreign demand for exports may, under our assumptions, even *lower* the physical volume of exports. This is seen to occur whenever the demand elasticity for imports is less than unity and $R$ consequently assumes negative values.[14] The consequences of increased demand for exports depend on the demand elasticity of imports as follows (all changes refer to the physical volume of exports and imports):

a) Exports rise by the same amount as imports when $\epsilon = \infty$ $(R = 1)$.
b) Exports rise by less than imports whenever $1 < \epsilon < \infty$ $(0 < R < 1)$.
c) Exports remain constant while imports rise when $\epsilon = 1$ $(R = 0)$.
d) Exports fall while imports rise whenever $\epsilon < 1$ $(R < 0)$.
e) Exports fall in proportion to the appreciation of the currency while imports remain unchanged when the demand elasticity of imports is zero.

[14] This result appears to be a fairly unrealistic possibility, but it is a necessary consequence of even slightly inelastic demand. The elasticity may still be substantially above a value that would be required to make a (small) devaluation of an administered exchange rate an ineffective tool for an improvement of balance-of-payments difficulties.

[ 97 ]

The real-income effect induced by the terms-of-trade change and the direct foreign-trade effect on the national income work against each other, and it appears at first glance that the ultimate outcome is uncertain. It is easy to show, however, that an unambiguous conclusion holds: the depressive foreign-trade effect will always dominate as long as the domestic elasticity of demand for imports is less than infinite. This is also the result at which Laursen and Metzler arrived.[15]

We shall examine three borderline cases.

$$\epsilon = 0 \quad \text{(Case } [e] \text{ above):}$$

The volume of imports does not change, while that of exports falls in proportion to the appreciation of the exchange rate. The adverse effect of the fall in exports could be counterbalanced only by an equal or greater increase in real domestic absorption. Expenditure on imports has fallen in proportion to the appreciation or, alternatively, by the same amount by which the physical volume of exports has fallen. To compensate for the fall in real national income owing to the lower export volume (always assuming unchanged prices of domestic production), expenditure on domestic output would have to rise by the same amount by which expenditure on imports has fallen. Condition (5) tells us, however, that appreciation and the consequent fall in the domestic price level *reduces* aggregate money expenditure on consumption. A compensating variation of sufficient magnitude in the consumption of domestic output is therefore precluded, and the over-all effect of the rise in foreign demand must be depressive.

$$\epsilon = 1 \quad \text{(Case } [c] \text{ above):}$$

Real national product cannot be affected by exports, since their physical volume does not change. The currency appreciates also in this case, and result (5) again implies that aggregate money expenditure on consumption is reduced. With an import demand elasticity of 1, total expenditure on imports remains constant, and the incidence of the reduction in aggregate consumer spending falls exclusively on domestic output. Under our assumption that prices of domestic products are rigid, real national income must also fall in this case.

$$\epsilon = \infty \quad \text{(Case } [a] \text{ above):}$$

[15] "Flexible Exchange Rates and the Theory of Employment," p. 299.

[ 98 ]

As has already been pointed out, this is the only instance in which the national income is not affected. No direct foreign-trade effect occurs, since exports and imports increase by the same amount; the real-income effect on consumption is absent because the exchange rate remains unchanged.

In all but the last one of the three limiting cases, the increase in foreign demand was seen to be followed by a contraction of domestic national income. It follows from continuity considerations that the same must hold for all intermediate values of the demand elasticity for imports. Infinite elasticity of demand for imports can be dismissed as a realistic possibility. Strictly Keynesian assumptions leave us, indeed, with the result that under flexible exchanges and in the absence of capital transfers a boom in one country will lower national incomes and employment in the rest of the world. Only a drastic modification of the initial assumptions can be expected to reverse the outcome.

An interesting corollary deserves brief mention. With pegged exchange rates, the increase in imports induced by an expansion of a country's national income acts as a leakage of effective demand, as is well known. Under flexible exchanges and forced equality of export and import values, the increased demand for imports during a boom serves as an additional expansionary factor. An upward shift of import demand will result in a rise or a fall in the physical volume of imports, depending on whether foreign demand for the country's exports is elastic or inelastic. The physical volume of exports, on the other hand, increases as long as the elasticity of foreign demand is above zero. With elastic (but not perfectly elastic) foreign demand, the rise in the export volume must always exceed that of imports. It follows that the induced increase in import demand will, through its effect on exports, further raise the national income of the expanding economy, under our assumptions.

Apart from its theoretical interest, too much should not be made of the Laursen-Metzler effect. The most unrealistic assumption that was made is undoubtedly the one postulating instantaneous balancing of the current account at every instant. Even for the very short run, some relief from the depressive effects of appreciation is brought about by the incipient financing which is the normal custom in international business transactions. A positive trade balance during the period immediately following an increase in the demand for a country's exports will occur and is likely to outweigh any adverse effects for some time.[16] Over the long run, the outcome depends on the direction taken by autonomous capital movements. The absence of trade imbalances was postulated here, as well as in the article by Laursen and Metzler on which our analysis is based, only in order to make it possible to analyze one effect at a time.[17] The preceding chapters should have demonstrated that exchange-rate flexibility in no way implies instantaneous balancing of the current account at all times.

Let us return to the analysis of previous chapters for a clue concerning the most probable direction of (net) capital movements in the case discussed above. If the expectation that the depreciation of the expanding country's currency is only a temporary matter dominates, speculators will tend to move funds there. This induces an export surplus for the appreciating country, a factor that counteracts the depressive Laursen-Metzler effect (provided that, as would normally have to be expected, the monetary impact of the capital transfer is not too important in comparison with the direct income effects) and possibly overcompensates for it. Expansion in the world at large is the result, as in a system of rigid prices and pegged exchange rates. Assuming that capital movements are unimpeded, can this outcome be expected to be the "normal" one?

The answer obviously hinges on the policies pursued by the countries concerned. If these policies are designed to eliminate any long-term trend in exchange rates, the answer is affirmative. For while speculators may, in the face of uncertain expectations, exhibit destabilizing inclinations in the short run, appropriate forward operations by the central bank[18] can always force them into line

[16] This point has been made by White in his criticism of the original article, "A Comment on Professors Laursen and Metzler," n. 8.

[17] Certain passages in the Laursen-Metzler article (e.g., p. 291) tend to convey the impression that the view of exchange-rate flexibility as an insulator against the international transmission of business cycles is at least partially wrong. When capital movements are not, as the authors assume, strictly prohibited, appropriate monetary policies can in the short run always channel capital transfers in the direction required to bring about the correct level of effective demand. It is this emancipation (at least in the short run) of domestic monetary policies from the dictates of events abroad, rather than a belief that the national income would not be affected as long as the values of imports and exports remain in balance, that presumably prompted most supporters of flexible rates to claim that flexibility could facilitate the preservation of full employment.

[18] See chap. iv above.

without difficulty and will inflict heavy losses on those who are obstinate enough to refuse. Given a prospect of stability over the long run, non-speculative long-term capital movements will in all probability conform to the same pattern. Profitable investment opportunities become more abundant in the expanding economy and interest rates are liable to rise. Rational behavior would consequently dictate a flow of both long-term investment capital ("direct" as well as "indirect") and speculative funds toward the country with the (momentarily) depreciated currency. The result is that the qualitative effect of changes in aggregate demand in one country on the national incomes of other countries is indeed the traditionally accepted one also under a flexible exchange-rate system, although part of the shock that would occur under pegged rates is absorbed by the exchange-rate adjustment. To repeat, all this depends on policies that prevent (or at least convincingly *appear* to prevent) an irreversible one-way movement of fluctuating rates. Once this premise is dropped, no definite conclusions are possible.

# VI

## *Currency Depreciation—a Cause of Inflation?*

In taking the step from the present system to a regime of universally flexible exchange rates, the currencies of many countries would undergo depreciation. One popular argument against devaluation of pegged rates has been that it would entail a rise in the price level for the countries concerned.[1] Wage-earners could be expected to press for higher wages. Unlikely to be resisted too strongly, the inflationary forces would gather momentum and soon lead to about the same degree of overvaluation that used to exist before.

I have shown elsewhere that devaluation need not be inflationary and that the very opposite is a definite possibility in many cases.[2] Since the question is obviously relevant to our topic, the argument will be briefly summarized. The presumption that prices may fall in most countries with overvalued currencies after the universal adoption of floating exchange rates is, as we shall observe, considerably stronger than in the case of devaluation by a single country. To fix ideas, we shall discuss the issue with reference to devaluation in a system of pegged rates.

The statement of the traditional view would probably start with

[1] Sir Roy Harrod has been one of the most articulate defenders of the view that devaluation is necessarily an inflationary factor. Whatever one may think of the issue, most people will be inclined to disagree with his suggestion that the increase in the price of postage stamps by the British postal authorities in 1957 was "a clear effect of the devaluation" of 1949. R. F. Harrod, *The Pound Sterling, 1951–1958* ("Essays in International Finance," No. 30 [Princeton: Princeton University Press, 1958]), p. 10.

[2] "The Effect of Devaluation on the Price Level," *Quarterly Journal of Economics,* **72** (May, 1958), 273–83; together with "Comments" by R. Hinshaw and J. Vanek, *ibid.,* November, 1958, pp. 614–32.

the assertion that domestic prices of imports must rise after devaluation. This would be correct if commodities could at all times move across international boundaries unimpeded by restrictions, no matter what exchange rate is in effect at any moment. In equilibrium, the domestic prices of imports would, apart from transport costs, equal their foreign prices multiplied by the exchange rate. Devaluation increases the rate (which we have defined as the unit price of foreign currency), and import prices must rise.

In practice, one essential prerequisite for this result is almost universally violated: the absence of trade restrictions in countries with overvalued currencies. Only unlimited availability of accommodating capital would make it possible to finance, over an extended period, the trade imbalance caused by an arbitrarily given degree of overvaluation. The maximum deficit on current account with which a country is able to live without facing the danger of default within a few months is usually rather limited. Experience has shown that even an apparently quite moderate deviation from the true equilibrium rate of exchange generally makes it necessary to play the full register of trade restrictions, predominantly exchange controls and quotas. Whenever such interference occurs, domestic and foreign prices are no longer equilibrated on the basis of the prevailing exchange rate. While any restraint of trade tends to improve a country's terms of trade, i.e., to lower the prices in the rest of the world of its imports relative to those of exports, it has the *opposite* effect on relative prices in the domestic economy. Internal prices of imports usually rise after restrictions are imposed, or producers would never have lobbied for protective tariffs and quotas. By the same token, removal of import controls, made possible by devaluation, must *lower* import prices, in spite of the optical illusion that a less "favorable" exchange rate always tends to raise them. It would seem that many writers have gone astray on this first step already.[3]

While the removal of trade restrictions by itself is deflationary, the ultimate effect on the price level need not be the same. From

[3] Notable exceptions are Ragnar Nurkse in League of Nations, *International Currency Experience* (1944), p. 167; R. Hinshaw, "Currency Appreciation as an Anti-Inflationary Device," *Quarterly Journal of Economics*, Vol. 65 (1951), "Final Comment," *ibid.*, Vol. 66 (1952); and esp. E. M. Bernstein, "Strategic Factors in Balance of Payments Adjustment," *International Monetary Fund Staff Papers*, 5 (1956), esp. 166–68.

the export sector, inflationary forces will emanate when a currency is devalued. By reducing foreign prices of exports, depreciation stimulates expansion in the export sector and tends to raise the domestic prices of typical export commodities. Increased demand for resources and the rise in disposable income in the export sector may cause price increases in other industries as well.

It is impossible to evaluate the combined result of these conflicting forces without more detailed information on their relative importance. Widespread unemployment, for example, makes it possible to expand production considerably without a significant price rise. It is obvious in this case that the general price level may fall after devaluation if the reduction of import prices goes far enough. This possibility might have been of some interest in the thirties, when governments used competitive devaluation as a remedy for unemployment. It is almost perplexing to note how fundamentally things have changed since then. There has not been one single instance since World War II in which a country would have undertaken devaluation with the intention of curing a slump. The typical picture has been the exact opposite. Economies have bumped against capacity barriers over an extended period before reluctant governments decided to adjust exchange rates toward the estimated value of their depreciated currencies.

It is more realistic under present conditions to assume full employment at all times. The reader will note that we thereby stack the cards *against* the possibility that devaluation may exert deflationary pressure. Bias in the same direction is achieved by the assumption of perfect competition in the domestic economy which we shall adopt. Where imperfect markets are sheltered from foreign competitors, the removal of trade barriers after devaluation tends to improve resource allocation and to put downward pressure on prices. This factor is likely to be particularly important in smaller countries whose tiny domestic markets limit the number of competitors in any industry.

Devaluation is usually undertaken with the intention of removing, or at least reducing, a deficit in the current account. Other things being equal, an improvement in the foreign balance is an inflationary factor. Resources previously absorbed by the domestic economy are made available to the rest of the world when a previous import surplus decreases. To avoid confusion, we shall first assume

[ 104 ]

that no change occurs in the balance on current account.[4] It may be objected that a discussion of devaluation under the assumption of a constant foreign balance is question-begging. A meaningful comparison of aggregate price levels in the two situations before and after devaluation would be impossible without this assumption, however. It is not difficult to convince oneself that it is, contrary to first impressions, an eminently realistic assumption. The determination of the size of a country's trade deficit is hardly ever the free choice of its government. At a time when the balance of payments is seriously adverse, foreign-exchange reserves are usually below their normal level. Whether or not the currency is devalued, the available reserves will impose a definite constraint on the external accounts. If, for whatever reasons, an exchange-rate adjustment is refused, the authorities will have to hold down imports by other means, presumably by direct controls of various kinds. On the other hand, even though a flexible rate may tend to depreciate, the authorities are free to deplete their foreign-exchange reserves, as long as they last, at a rate of their own choosing. They may thus, if they want, preserve the magnitude of the previous deficit and prevent the inflationary impact of a balance-of-payments improvement after the restoration of flexibility.

It is true that governments may often have obtained additional emergency loans or grants from abroad in view of their country's imminent failure to pay for imports. It is also understandable that they should have sought to explain their predicament as an irreparable disequilibrium which traditional policies could not hope to correct and that they have often succeeded in this attempt. Foreign assistance solicited in this way has undoubtedly often made possible additional imports, by themselves a deflationary factor.[5]

The analysis of earlier chapters has emphasized another important factor. Overvaluation inevitably repels much of the autonomous private capital inflow that might otherwise occur. It

[4] As in the rest of this study, the foreign balance is understood to be measured in terms of foreign currency. Changes in the exchange rate could otherwise give rise to ambiguity whenever the initial balance differs from zero.

[5] Aid to less advanced countries has become a generally accepted practice. A case can be made for the view that the equity considerations that have led to the progressive income tax in all advanced countries should apply equally well to the world at large. Gunnar Myrdal, among others, has taken this stand in *An International Economy* (New York: Harper, 1956). But the issue should not be blurred with imagined difficulties.

may very well be that governmental grants induced by chronic deficits have in many instances fallen short of the volume of normal private capital flows lost through currency overvaluation. Far from forcing a country to tighten its belt, devaluation to the equilibrium level with a subsequent prospect of stability would even permit a *rise* in the permissible trade deficit under these circumstances.

So much for justifying the realism of our initial assumptions. The heart of the matter is a simple index-number theorem that may be stated as follows: The aggregate price level in an economy, measured in terms of any one of the accepted varieties of index numbers (with the exception of Laspeyres' index which may remain constant), must fall when an unambiguous increase in real national income (measured in terms of the usual indices) occurs while the money value of domestic absorption remains constant.

As set out in detail in the Appendix, we shall say that an unambiguous increase in real income has occurred whenever the two inequalities[6]

$$\Sigma P_2 Q_2 \geqq \Sigma P_2 Q_1 , \qquad (1)$$

and

$$\Sigma P_1 Q_2 > \Sigma P_1 Q_1$$

are fulfilled, where subscripts *1* denote the initial position, and subscripts *2* the situation after the change. Constancy of the money value of domestic absorption is expressed as

$$\Sigma P_1 Q_1 = \Sigma P_2 Q_2 . \qquad (2)$$

When the first inequality in (1) is divided by $\Sigma P_1 Q_1$, the second one into $\Sigma P_2 Q_2$, we obtain, using condition (2),

$$\frac{\Sigma P_2 Q_1}{\Sigma P_1 Q_1} \leqq 1 , \quad \text{and} \quad \frac{\Sigma P_2 Q_2}{\Sigma P_1 Q_2} < 1 . \qquad (3)$$

The first fraction is Laspeyres' price index, the second Paasche's. Paasche's index indicates a fall in the price level after the improvement; Laspeyres' index likewise records a fall, or at least constancy.

[6] There is admittedly an element of arbitrariness in this definition. Any macroeconomic welfare criterion can indicate only *potential* improvements as long as we do not know whether a given change is accompanied by a suitable redistribution of incomes to guarantee an actual improvement in accordance with the interpersonal welfare judgments the society—or its dictator, or ruling body— has chosen to adopt.

As long as the money value of the country's domestic absorption remains constant, we conclude that devaluation can result in an unambiguous rise in the aggregate price level only if both inequalities in (1) above are violated. If the balance on current account shows a substantial improvement, there is a legitimate presumption that they may be violated, for the drain on the country's resources decreases the volume of commodities available for domestic use. In addition, the improvement in the foreign balance tends to raise money incomes; the implied violation of condition (2) strengthens the inflationary forces.

But when the foreign balance remains unchanged, the opposite presumption is plausible. It is likely that absorption does not change in this case, so that condition (2) is satisfied. The removal of import restrictions after devaluation tends to increase the volume of trade in both directions. Subject to the usual qualifications (perfect competition, absence of external economies), reallocation of production according to the principle of comparative advantage implies a presumption that both inequalities (1) are fulfilled. Only one factor may reverse this conclusion: the possibly adverse terms-of-trade effect of trade liberalization. If foreign demand is relatively inelastic, a country may gain from the imposition of limited controls.[7] Conversely, their removal must then entail a loss.

As a purely theoretical matter, the possibility that a rise in the price level may result from a pronounced terms-of-trade effect cannot be denied. This argument lies on an entirely different plane from those usually heard, however. Most economists are inclined to discount the relevance of the terms-of-trade argument as far as tariffs are concerned. For those who do, there is no justification for taking the opposite stand on the issue discussed here.

If the index-number inequalities (3) are fulfilled when the trade balance remains constant, the price level will still fall, even when the balance improves. The improvement cannot exceed a certain level, of course, as should be sufficiently clear.

Another qualification must be added. The index-number argument used above, as well as the principle of comparative advantage that underlies it, involves comparisons of different positions of general equilibrium. Before all variables have had time to swing into equilibrium after a given change, the Laspeyres index

[7] See the Appendix for details.

may indicate a price rise while the Paasche index falls.[8] In view of the labor involved in constructing base weights, continuously recorded time series of the price level are invariably of the Laspeyres type. Empirical data are consequently biased toward indicating a rise in the price level or toward understating a fall when a gain in real income is achieved. In addition, the rise in potential welfare that occurs when new commodities, previously not available, are imported after the removal of import restrictions goes entirely unrecorded.

The recorded price-level changes after devaluation of a single overvalued currency are at least uncertain, therefore, unless the improvement in the trade balance is quite substantial. What outcome can be expected when all overvalued currencies simultaneously depreciate and these countries liberalize trade after the adoption of a universal system of flexible exchanges?

From the effect on the terms of trade, a deflationary tendency appears less likely. Reciprocal demand by the rest of the world facing a group of countries will be less elastic than for a single country. The over-all deterioration of their terms of trade vis-à-vis all other countries will therefore generally be more noticeable. It seems plausible, however, that another factor is far more important. Currency overvaluation is usually accompanied by a tightening of trade restrictions generally, not only for imports from the countries whose currencies appear "hardest" under the given system of par values. Although discrimination against hard-currency countries will inevitably be more pronounced, experience has amply demonstrated how drastically the aggregate volume of trade shrinks even between countries whose currencies are, to all appearances, about equally overvalued with respect to "hard" currencies. As exchange flexibility restores equilibrium rates, multilateral abolition of controls becomes possible. The larger the number of economically independent countries in the previously overvalued block, the more the welfare effects of increased trade will make themselves felt, and the more likely is a general downward movement of prices.

We notice a straightforward corollary of the results derived above. Tightening of import controls as a substitute for devaluation will only *accentuate* an existing inflationary trend once the controls

---

[8] For details of the argument, see my "Reply," *Quarterly Journal of Economics*, **72** (November, 1958), 627–29.

exceed the (vaguely defined) "optimum" level.[9] Most of the literature has argued the reverse: that direct controls are often the only realistic choice because devaluation is an inflationary factor that would defeat its own purpose before too long. The invalidity of this view is clearly revealed when it is carried to its logical conclusion: if true, the price level would always have to fall whenever a pegged exchange rate is adjusted so as to make a currency more overvalued. The price level would reach the attainable minimum (and, given the implied connection with the index-number criteria, real income would attain a maximum) once the exchange rate reaches the point when *all exports have ceased.*

There is an obvious answer to those who consider the terms-of-trade argument (as we have seen, the only valid qualification of our conclusion that devaluation of an overvalued currency may be used to *de*flate the price level) persuasive enough to doubt the wisdom of introducing exchange-rate flexibility for overvalued currencies. Supply and demand elasticities differ widely for different commodities. Judicious selection of tariff rates could take the maximum possible advantage of such differences even while exchange rates fluctuate freely. Exchange controls, on the other hand, are usually imposed across the board, with little hope that the optimum pattern of discrimination will be approached. On the contrary, they always discriminate against luxuries whose demand elasticities are likely to exceed those of necessities and thus take minimum advantage of the potential gains from distorting the terms of trade.[10]

The issue discussed here illustrates another one of the serious

[9] See the Appendix on the indeterminacy of the "optimum tariff."

[10] We may briefly mention another consideration that is by no means novel but rarely heeded in shaping policy. The entry of foreign luxuries is often impeded while no restraints are imposed on the *consumption* of domestically produced substitutes. The only result is a premium on the production of luxury items, while the producers of vital necessities are offered relatively low incentives. The obvious, but rarely practiced, policy for a country in difficulties would be a stiff penalty on domestic consumption of whatever commodities are considered nonessential, whether they originate at home or abroad. But even when this is not done, the principle of comparative advantage still dictates unrestricted imports of *all* commodities (barring the ever-present qualifications concerning terms of trade and infant industries). Economic loss must result from the diversion of domestic resources to the production of nonessential goods that could be imported at bargain prices in exchange for exports of domestically produced "essentials."

[ 109 ]

fallacies to which the unguarded use of income analysis easily leads. For the mind steeped in national-income aggregates, the possibility that a situation with an (algebraically) smaller import surplus can, with constant technology and unchanged employment level, involve a higher real income for the community must remain a mystery.[11] Only classical general-equilibrium theory will make it possible to appreciate the fact that an improvement in the trade balance is not necessarily equivalent to a welfare loss during the current period.

We should also beware of one possible macroeconomic misinterpretation of the unorthodox effect of devaluation on the price level pointed out here. Restrictions raise domestic prices of imports and those importers who are lucky enough to receive the license allocations reap windfall profit rates unless the licenses are auctioned off. But it does not follow that a possible fall in the price level of imports after devaluation depends on the extent to which excess profits of importers are eliminated. Under the import restrictions, importers earn higher unit profits on a *reduced volume* of trade, and their aggregate income may well be below the level it would attain under freer trade.

Only superficially does it appear as if the existence of price controls on imports could change our conclusions. The opportunity to purchase a limited value of imports at lower than equilibrium prices releases purchasing power that will presumably be directed toward other commodities. Given a constant level of aggregate money expenditure, the induced rise in the prices of domestically produced commodities must compensate for the artificially low prices of imports. *General* price controls, in effect before and after devaluation, do not change our conclusions in a foreseeable way. If general price controls are removed simultaneously with the devaluation, the officially registered price level may well rise, although the index-number comparisons would indicate a fall *if* equilibrium prices were used for both commodity bundles. It need not be shown in detail that the registered rise in the price level cannot be used as an argument against devaluation and/or for general price controls under these circumstances.

[11] Even as careful an author as H. G. Johnson writes: "If the economy is already fully employed, however, the additional output required cannot be provided by increasing production; it can only be provided through a reduction in the previous level of real expenditure." *International Trade and Economic Growth* (London: Allen & Unwin, 1958), p. 165.

Contrary to common belief, apparently deflationary effects of devaluation are by no means an unusual phenomenon. They have, of course, often been swamped by continuing inflation that had originally made exchange-rate adjustment inevitable. This is a plausible interpretation of the consequences of the British devaluation of 1949, for example. An objective appraisal is made almost impossible in this case in view of the world-wide inflationary tendencies caused by the beginning of the Korean War only nine months later. Until then, the general upward trend of British prices did not seem to be very much affected by the devaluation. For another empirical example, the reader is referred to the discussion of the Austrian devaluation of 1953 in my "Reply," pp. 631–32. The Austrian price level remained practically constant, although all other forces would have favored a rise, among them a sharp reduction of the previously substantial import surplus, a deterioration of the terms of trade by 13 per cent, and an expansionary monetary policy that brought about an increase in the money supply by 20 per cent while employment and the real gross national product according to the national-accounting definition remained virtually unchanged.[12]

[12] It is one consequence of the phenomena discussed in this chapter and the Appendix that the real national product as measured in a country's national accounts may very well remain unchanged while the "real" national product that could serve as a true indicator of potential welfare would rise, given the qualitative improvement in the available product mix through more intensive international trade. This subtle ambiguity of the usual measure of real national product arises from the fact that this measure is obtained through dividing a nominal-value index by price indices of the Laspeyres type, and is therefore a quantity index of the Paasche type. It follows from the analysis of section 3 of the Appendix that Paasche quantity indices understate the true increase of potential welfare and may possibly even record a *fall* instead.

# VII

## The Case against Pegged Exchange Rates

Under the *Articles of Agreement* of the International Monetary Fund, each member country is required to announce a par value for its currency with respect to all other currencies (Art. IV, sec. 1). Of immediate interest are the following additional provisions:

Art. IV, sec. 3: The maximum and the minimum rates for exchange transactions between the currencies of members taking place within their territories shall not differ from parity
  (i) in the case of spot exchange transactions, by more than one %;
  (ii) in the case of other exchange transactions, by a margin which exceeds the margin for spot exchange transactions by more than the Fund considers reasonable.

Art. IV, sec. 5: (a) A member shall not propose a change in the par value of its currency except to correct a fundamental disequilibrium.

  (b) A change in the par value of a member's currency may be made only on the proposal of the member and only after consultation with the Fund.

  (c) When a change is proposed, the Fund shall first take into account the changes, if any, which have already taken place in the initial par value of the member's currency, as determined under Article XX, section 4. If the proposed change, together with all previous changes, whether increases or decreases,
    (i) does not exceed ten percent of the initial par value, the Fund shall raise no objection;
    (ii) does not exceed a further ten per cent of the initial par value, the Fund may either concur or

[ 112 ]

object, but shall declare its attitude within
seventy-two hours if the member so requests;

(iii) is not within (i) or (ii) above, the Fund may
either concur or object, but shall be entitled to
a longer period in which to declare its attitude.

. . . . . . . . . . . . . . . . . . . .

(f) The Fund shall concur in a proposed change which
is within the terms of (c) (ii) or (c) (iii) above if it is
satisfied that the change is necessary to correct a
fundamental disequilibrium.

It is generally agreed today that the Fund has not, with the possible exception of the last few years, fulfilled the high hopes placed in it at the time of its creation. What it lacks is perhaps better appreciated if one of the requirements that Keynes apparently considered essential is recalled:

1. (d) We need a system possessed of an internal stabilizing mechanism,
by which pressure is exercised on any country whose balance of
payments with the rest of the world is departing from equilibrium
in either direction, so as to prevent movements which must create
for its neighbors an equal but opposite want of balance.[1]

The automaticity of the adjustment mechanism visualized by Keynes appears to conflict with another one of his recommendations:

(1) There should be the least possible interference with internal national
policies, and the plan should not wander from the international
*terrain.* . . . In the realm of internal policy, the authority of the
governing board of the proposed institution should be limited to
recommendations, or, at most, to imposing conditions for more extended enjoyment of the facilities which the institution offers.

(2) The technique of the plan must be capable of application irrespective
of the type and principle of government and the economic policy
existing in the prospective member States.[2]

The removal of the internal policies of member countries from the direct influence of the Fund necessarily requires adjustment by variables outside the realm of genuinely "internal" policies if some automaticity of balance-of-payments adjustment is desired.

[1] *Proposals for an International Clearing Union* (London: H.M. Stationery Office, Cmd. 6437, April 7, 1943); reprinted in *Federal Reserve Bulletin,* **29,** No. 6, (1943), 509.

[2] *Proposals; Federal Reserve Bulletin,* p. 508.

The only variables that meet this specification would appear to be exchange rates between currencies. In principle, alterations of exchange rates were not meant to be precluded by the *Articles of Agreement*. The *Articles* permit par value changes in order to cure a "fundamental disequilibrium." The term has, incidentally, never been officially defined. Experience has amply shown that discontinuous par value changes are a poor method for maintaining equilibrium in international payments. Frequent adjustments of par values are discouraged by the *Articles of Agreement;* infrequent change, on the other hand, implies that every alteration is likely to be preceded by a major and prolonged maladjustment. The serious balance-of-payments deficits which arise in such cases cannot always be fully bridged by international loans. Almost inevitably they have to be accompanied by exchange controls and other restrictions of foreign trade. The presence of such restrictions in the majority of countries has characterized most of the postwar era. The painful losses they have caused through misallocation of the world's resources have only become fully apparent after the relaxation of trade restrictions in recent years.

The exacting standards of monetary and fiscal policies imposed by the technique of pegged exchange rates—if it is to be workable at all—should by now have become obvious. If the limits of variability are as narrow as they used to be under the gold standard, pegged exchange rates make the currencies of all participating countries as effectively one as gold-standard currencies were made into one international currency. Truly independent monetary policies by member countries are precluded. Many governments have nevertheless been tempted to take the absence of prescribed rituals in the event of a deficit in the foreign balance as a license to conduct their domestic policies without, or with only little, consideration for international repercussions. The charge is not entirely groundless that post-Keynesian economics has developed with a built-in bias toward the unrealistic model of an economy in isolation and that many of its policy recommendations tended to disregard effects on a country's foreign balance. The attempts to make a virtue out of a necessity, and to defend trade restrictions because the theoretical possibility of gains for the country imposing restrictions can be demonstrated, were perhaps also more frequent than usual. Without going into a detailed discussion of these matters—some of which are touched upon elsewhere in this book—attention is called to the fact, perhaps not purely accidental, that postwar growth was, by and large, most impressive not in those countries where stringent exchange controls had to be imposed as a result of currency over-valuation but rather in the countries with relatively liberal trade policies. The rest of this chapter will emphasize primarily the problems and disadvantages that arise from currency *over*valuation, although there must necessarily be undervalued currencies for every overvalued one.

Readers may perhaps feel inclined to object that the possibility of making pegged rates true equilibrium rates through appropriate policies is underemphasized unfairly. The principal target for attack in this chapter is indeed the preservation of maladjusted rates and not so much pegged exchange rates as such. It is true that universal willingness to conduct strong policies in order to make pegged rates realistic and maintainable without exchange controls does not seem such a forlorn hope now as it appeared to be only a few years ago. Against this, however, stands the opposite experience of many years, as well as the fact that nobody can guarantee eternal willingness of all governments to subordinate their domestic affairs to economic developments abroad, even if such willingness should ever become universal at some day in the future. Moreover, if all countries were prepared to conduct their economic policies so as to make pegged rates long-run equilibrium rates at all times, pegging would become superfluous anyway, since fluctuating rates would also be highly stable.[3] Finally, as discussed at length in chapter iv, fluctuating rates can perform a most vital function in facilitating counter-cyclical policies. Perhaps somewhat paradoxically, governments can be expected to be all the more successful in achieving long-run stability of exchange rates if they let them fluctuate freely and attempt to promote exchange-rate stability through means other than direct intervention in the exchange markets.

In recent years, the administrators of the International Monetary Fund have tended to take the ban on fluctuating exchange rates im-

---

[3] This has sometimes been used as an argument *against* the introduction of flexible exchange rates. See, e.g., L. Robbins, "The International Economic Problem," *Lloyds Bank Review*, January, 1953, p. 16. The preference for pegged rates under conditions where freely fluctuating rates would also be highly stable endows the former with a superiority a priori for which there is no other justification but mere habit. The last point above is the most persuasive argument against this line of reasoning.

plied in its *Articles of Agreement* less and less seriously. The opposition to Canada's decision to make the Canadian dollar a fluctuating currency, as reflected, though with diplomatic restraint, in the International Monetary Fund's *Annual Report* for 1951, pp. 36–41, gave way to the scarcely disguised indorsement of the Argentine experiment in December, 1958.[4]

1

## THE SIGNIFICANCE OF EQUILIBRIUM EXCHANGE RATES

The central argument in favor of flexible exchanges is identical with the traditional case for free trade. This wider significance of exchange-rate policy has, unfortunately, been neglected all too frequently. In many instances, the battle has been fought over narrow technical matters more worthy of the attention of bank accountants than of economists.

As was demonstrated in chapter i, at least one exchange rate that guarantees a statically stable equilibrium in the foreign-exchange market must exist at every instant between the currencies of any two trading countries.[5] The attainment of this exchange-rate value at any moment in time permits the removal of all those restrictions on trade and capital movements that are invariably associated with the rationing of foreign exchange when the rate is pegged at a disequilibrium level. There is a presumption that the system comprising both economies moves "closer" to the Pareto-optimum corresponding to the given state of the arts, the distribution of resources, and the tastes of all individuals whenever restrictions are removed. Such "closeness" is, of course, not operationally measurable. As a purely theoretical matter, the persistence of other violations of optimum conditions, always inevitable in the real world, even makes it possible for elimination of exchange controls to move the economy away from the optimum.[6] Purists may be in-

[4] International Monetary Fund, *International Financial News Survey*, January 9, 1959.

[5] Although the existence of more than one stable equilibrium cannot be excluded on purely theoretical grounds, the consequences are so much at odds with experience that it would appear relatively safe to exclude it as an empirical possibility. See chapter i for details.

[6] Cf. R. G. Lipsey and R. K. Lancaster, "The General Theory of Second Best," *Review of Economic Studies*, 24 (1956–57), 11–32. The concept of "second

clined to castigate the pragmatic view that the usual and over-whelming presumption must be the opposite. They may feel less comfortable in their position when it is pointed out that it implies acceptance of the discredited "principle of insufficient reason" that alternative events whose probability of occurrence is not known, or possibly not subject to quantitative measurement at all, must be taken to be equally likely.

Welfare gains through a closer approach to a Pareto-optimum may be overcompensated for by welfare losses owing to unfavorable income redistribution. This can be a valid argument against the elimination of trade restrictions *in general*, as opposed to changes in the degree of protection of particular commodities, only to the extent that controls benefit one country as a whole at the expense of another. Even if we accept the view that it is perfectly proper for a country to exploit the rest of the world, it must be stressed that it can do so much more effectively by the imposition of judiciously selected restrictions on particular commodities, provided it can be shown that other countries will not retaliate.

Barring convincing reasons to believe the contrary, it would therefore seem desirable to approach the equilibrium rate of ex-change as closely as possible at every instant. How good are the chances that an administered rate will be (and remain) pegged at precisely this value? In principle, any one of the infinity of exchange-rate values in the continuum of positive real numbers is eligible. Given a certain pattern of prices, incomes, and all other economic variables in the two countries at any moment, only one (or, at worst, a denumerable infinity) of these values will provide a stable equilibrium. The probability of hitting precisely this value when a number is chosen at random is zero.

The reader will perhaps be inclined to object that this reasoning is too facetious to be acceptable. He may argue that it is not the whole positive range of numbers that is ever considered, but, for all prac-tical purposes, only a relatively small interval somewhere in the neighborhood of the actual equilibrium rate. Even though it is practically certain that policymakers will never be able to estimate the correct equilibrium rate precisely, it might be argued that a small divergence from it does not really matter because the excess

---

best" solutions is extensively discussed in J. E. Meade, *Trade and Welfare* (London: Oxford University Press, 1955).

demand of foreign exchange is bound to be small in the neighborhood of the equilibrium rate. This is probably true for the excess demand derived from the market schedules on current account, but hardly so for that derived from capital movements. It is hardly proper to separate capital movements from a market which the ease and speed of transfer make so notoriously volatile. Speculative activity is bound to aggravate the disequilibrium if a pegged rate is just slightly out of line. Once holders of liquid funds realize that the administered rate overstates the long-run equilibrium value of a currency, and if they have reason to believe that the authorities are unwilling to impose the hardships of deflationary action merely to improve its rating on the exchanges—a very reasonable hypothesis in many instances—they can rest assured that the currency will not appreciate in the foreseeable future. Rational behavior dictates a transfer of funds abroad; the result is large-scale capital outflow if capital movements are free.

A flexible rate would adjust to the true equilibrium value and check the outflow of funds. If the central bank stands ready to defend the overvalued rate, the only consequence is a rapid depletion of its foreign-exchange reserves. As the reserves approach the vanishing point, the certainty that no appreciation can be expected gradually changes into a growing apprehension that eventual devaluation is inevitable. Bear speculators will sell domestic currency short on an increasing scale. As its forward value depreciates, covered interest arbitrage intensifies the pressure on the spot market and magnifies the drain on the country's foreign-exchange reserves. Additional disturbances arise from "leads and lags" in payments for exports and imports. Experience has shown that they make themselves felt with remarkable speed even in the presence of all-embracing controls over capital movements.[7] A definite constraint is imposed on the continuation of this process by the size of the country's reserves unless an autonomous change makes the equilibrium value of the currency appreciate to or above the pegged rate. No convincing reason justifies the belief that random shocks of the required intensity will always be supplied at the right time, nor do the observed facts of recent history offer much encouragement.

[7] See S. I. Katz, "Leads and Lags in Sterling Payments," *Review of Economics and Statistics*, Vol. 35 (1953).

The answer to the dilemma was usually not sought in immediate devaluation as soon as it became apparent that the announced parity overstated the true value of a currency. Such a measure would run counter to the basic philosophy of the International Monetary Fund. Governments have, as a matter of fact, stuck to the principle of exchange-rate rigidity with much greater tenacity than the Fund itself. Irrational motives play their part. Devaluation may be seen as a disturbing reflection on a country's honor and its international standing, or the monetary authority may regard it as an embarrassing admission of failure in its task of safeguarding stability of prices and incomes.

A valid objection to frequent adjustments of pegged exchange rates is that they would effectively wreck the avowed purpose of the system, the elimination of exchange risks for commercial trade and international investment. The disturbances caused by the discrete changes characteristic of the "adjustable peg" are considerably more serious than those provoked by the smooth, day-to-day fluctuations in a system of fluctuating rates. Even though changes occur less frequently, they are bound to be much larger, and the exact time of their incidence must necessarily remain secret. The degree to which exporters, importers, and international lenders can protect themselves from large windfall losses owing to sudden and drastic exchange-rate adjustment depends on their dexterity in outguessing the forced lies of ministers of finance and chancellors of the exchequer. The British devaluation of 1949 is an outstanding case in point. Only lack of experience with a system of this kind can explain why such considerations escaped the attention of the drafters of the charter of the International Monetary Fund when they stipulated waiting periods of seventy-two hours and more for approval of parity changes, with the inevitable news leaks during extended deliberation of a large decision-making body.[8]

---

[8] *Articles of Agreement*, Art. IV, sec. 5 (see above). The "adjustable peg" has always been one of the principal bones of contention among supporters of flexible exchange rates. See F. D. Graham, *The Cause and Cure of "Dollar Shortage"* ("Essays in International Finance," No. 10 [Princeton: Princeton University Press, 1949]), pp. 8–9; J. E. Meade, *The Balance of Payments* (London: Oxford University Press, 1951), pp. 228–29; M. Friedman, *Essays in Positive Economics* (Chicago: University of Chicago Press, 1953), pp. 163–64; G. Haberler, *Currency Convertibility* (Washington: American Enterprise Association, 1954), pp. 24–25; F. A. Lutz, "The Case for Flexible Exchange Rates," *Banca Nazionale del Lavoro Quarterly Review*, No. 31 (December, 1954), pp. 175–

In practice, the remedy governments have almost invariably re-
sorted to when a currency became overvalued is a tightening of
exchange controls or other restrictions. It seems safe to argue that
uninterrupted freedom of *capital* movements, at the very least, is
likely to remain difficult to reconcile with universally pegged exchange rates, given the reluctance of many governments to subject
internal economic policies to the demands of balance-of-payments
equilibrium. On the other hand, it is hard to see how, without freedom of capital movements, international lending can possibly be
expected to attain the magnitude required for satisfactory growth
of the world's underdeveloped economies. The claim that rigid exchange rates are necessary for the promotion of international lending has, incidentally, usually been accepted as one of the more
convincing arguments in their favor.

The argument that exchange flexibility increases risk is just as
dubious when it is applied to the current account.[9] Administrators
of exchange controls have had ample opportunity to learn that enforcement of restrictions on capital movements is ineffectual unless
they are accompanied by an equally detailed supervision of commodity trade and invisible items. Exporters and importers whom
the pegging of exchange rates supposedly relieves from a substantial part of their trading risks see themselves forced to wrestle
with an intricate maze of regulations, many of which are subject to
sudden and arbitrary change. It is a moot question whether these
factors do not frequently impose more uncertainty and bothersome
impediments on their operations than the most erratic of exchange
fluctuations. Keynes, for one, has always disputed the notion that
exchange flexibility might seriously hamper foreign trade. In the
*Treatise*, besides emphasizing the hedging facilities offered by forward markets, Keynes pointed out that fluctuations of commodity

---

85; W. M. Scammell, *International Monetary Policy*, (London: Macmillan, 1957),
pp. 93–100.

Sir Donald MacDougall has aptly characterized this system when he said
that speculation under inflationary conditions "might be less serious than with
flexible rates," provided that "memories were not too long and speculators did
not look too far ahead." *The World Dollar Problem* (London: Macmillan, 1957),
p. 336. It is surprising that Sir Donald remains a solid supporter of a system
which he recognizes to rest on foundations as shaky as these.

[9] See R. Nurkse, *Conditions of International Monetary Equilibrium* ("Essays
in International Finance," No. 4 [Princeton: Princeton University Press, 1945]);
reprinted in *Readings in the Theory of International Trade*, pp. 5–6.

prices have often exhibited much wider amplitudes than those of exchange rates. In addition, he argued that "exchange fluctuations will be as likely—perhaps more likely—to compensate for these individual price fluctuations as to aggravate them."[10] Tsiang has called attention to the interesting fact that during the four years of freely fluctuating exchange rates prior to the restoration of the gold standard in the United Kingdom in April, 1925, the exchange rate of the pound sterling in terms of the U.S. dollar fluctuated less than either the domestic wholesale price index or the purchasing power parity of the pound in terms of the U.S. dollar (based on wholesale price indices of the two countries).[11]

It should not make too much difference whether a single or a multiple peg is established. A multiple exchange-rate system cannot ease the stresses and strains associated with disequilibrium rates, as the monetary authorities in many countries have had occasion to learn. The price discrimination implied by multiple rates is incompatible with optimal allocation of the world's resources, the main objective of universal currency convertibility. The usual pattern of multiple rates favors imports of necessities while penalizing imports of luxuries. A highly unwelcome effect on domestic resource allocation is all too frequently forgotten: the sectors producing luxury goods are artificially induced to expand while the production of necessities is curtailed.

A scheme of greater intuitive appeal is the establishment of a freely fluctuating exchange rate for capital transfers in conjunction with a pegged rate for all commercial transactions.[12] The rationale of this proposal is to impose as heavy a penalty as possible on

[10] *Treatise on Money* (New York: Harcourt, Brace, 1930), 2, 333.

[11] S. C. Tsiang, "Fluctuating Exchange Rates in Countries with Relatively Stable Economies: Some European Experiences After World War I," *International Monetary Fund Staff Papers*, 7 (October, 1959), 256. The three series are compared on the basis of the respective standard deviations from twelve-month moving averages, computed as 1.6 for the exchange rate, 2.5 for the wholesale price index, and 2.2 for the purchasing power parity.

[12] Arrangements of this kind have been in operation in a number of Latin-American countries after the war. They were first proposed by Robert Triffin in *International Monetary Policies* ("Postwar Economic Studies," No. 7 [Board of Governors, Federal Reserve System, September 1947]), pp. 69-75. Professor Triffin has, however, expressed a highly critical attitude toward multiple rates pegged at unrealistic levels. *Europe and the Money Muddle* (New Haven: Yale University Press, 1957), esp. p. 121, n. 21. See also E. R. Schlesinger, *Multiple*

capital flight that might be induced by a prospect of sustained inflation, while avoiding the deterioration in the country's terms of trade that would usually be associated with the depreciation of a single flexible rate brought about by massive capital flight.

There is little doubt that this compromise between exchange-rate flexibility and pegging is preferable to the rigidity of a single pegged rate. Quite apart from the greater administrative difficulties, however, the advantages of the scheme over a single flexible rate for *all* transactions are questionable. Flexibility solely for the exchange rate applicable to capital transfers would make a real difference only in an environment in which the public anticipates continued inflation. Whenever capital flight occurs on a large scale, this anticipation is usually only too well founded. Although the commercial exchange rate may initially be set at a level that guarantees stable equilibrium as far as purely commercial transactions (or perhaps these as well as long-term capital movements) are concerned,[13] it will not remain an equilibrium rate for very long under these circumstances. Once it ceases to be that, all our objections to pegged disequilibrium rates apply.

The "multiflex" system may be proposed, on the other hand, with the intention of eliminating temporary fluctuations of the exchange rate for current-account transactions while sufficiently strong measures are undertaken in order to forestall an irreversible deterioration of a country's currency in the long run. It is not necessarily true that exchange-rate oscillations are more harmful when they affect commodity trade and not only autonomous capital movements. The preservation of a favorable environment for the inflow of foreign capital may be a much more vital matter for many countries than the guaranty of exchange-rate rigidity for exporters and importers. Particularly for underdeveloped countries, there may therefore be just as strong a case for maximum stability of the exchange rate applicable to transactions on *capital* account while the commercial rate is left to fluctuate freely.

---

*Exchange Rates and Economic Development* ("Princeton Studies in International Finance," No. 2 [Princeton: Princeton University Press, 1952]), and V. Graden, "Effects of Multiple Exchange Rates," *Weltwirtschaftliches Archiv*, 81 (1958), 176–216.

[13] There is a valid objection, moreover, to the concept of an "equilibrium rate" that abstracts from all phenomena related to short-term capital movements, such as covered interest arbitrage.

## 2

## MONETARY POLICY UNDER PEGGED
## EXCHANGE RATES

Two sharply contradictory views are employed in defense of pegged exchanges: (1) Rather than achieving equilibrium in a country's external accounts through flexibility of the exchange rate, it is preferable to hold it stable and attempt to bring about the needed changes through flexibility of other variables. (2) The introduction of flexible exchanges is only practicable if the monetary and fiscal authorities stand ready to undertake the necessary measures to safeguard internal price and income stability. Since many governments do not seem to be prepared to do this, proposals to make exchange rates flexible are based on wishful thinking and must be dismissed as unrealistic.

Once the exchange rate has been pegged for good, internal prices and domestic absorption are the principal variables through which economic policy can attempt the balancing of a country's external accounts over the long run without seriously impairing the free flow of commodities and international lending. Maintenance of that flow at a high level is one of the avowed objectives of a regime of pegged exchanges. Yet price stability without interference with international trade requires precisely the strong monetary and fiscal policies that the view expressed in (2) above presents as an unattainable goal. While it is true that a weak monetary policy offers no particular advantages under flexible exchanges as well, it should be appreciated that it is a truly fixed exchange rate and not a flexible one that is most demanding for monetary management.[14] In the very short run, foreign-exchange reserves may serve as a buffer. As experience has shown, even a small divergence between peg and true equilibrium rate is liable to lead to their depletion in very little time if capital movements are free.

Possibly the most serious blow to the arguments under review is the conclusion we have reached in chapter iv. It was shown there that the potentially most forceful argument in favor of flexible rates is their role as a highly sensitive catalyst in making an econo-

[14] Keynes described the "technique of bank rate coupled with a rigid parity of the foreign exchanges" as "the most dangerous technique for the maintenance of equilibrium which can possibly be imagined." *The General Theory of Employment, Interest and Money* (New York: Harcourt, Brace, 1936), p. 339.

my responsive to monetary policy. Not only does a regime of pegged exchanges require a particularly determined monetary policy in order to be successful but it also deprives that policy of what is possibly the most promising tool available. The whole burden of adjustment to monetary stimuli is thrown on *domestic* absorption, whereas flexible exchanges would spread much, if not most, of it over the rest of the world. There is no need to argue the case that the domestic economy may only respond sluggishly to orthodox monetary measures. We have seen it argued by most writings on monetary theory and policy during the past twenty-five years.

Professors L. Robbins and J. Viner have registered their opposition to fluctuating rates on the tactical grounds that they would "remove the only restraint of any strength against marked inflation, namely, the widespread official and public dislike of exchange depreciation."[15] If events confirmed this fear, it would provide a potent objection. One can, however, argue equally convincingly that the instantaneous and publicly visible evidence of currency deterioration when exchange rates fluctuate freely may be an even more commanding inducement for governments to preserve monetary stability than the aversion against altering an adjustable peg. The latter measure can be, and usually is, postponed for a considerable length of time. The postwar experience would suggest that the possibility of fixing exchange rates by administrative decree, combined with exchange controls, has been one of the principal means of camouflaging inflationary pressure that would have become immediately apparent if exchange rates had been free to fluctuate.[16] The inflation argument, the merits of which can, after all, only be assessed on the basis of empirical evidence, is further weakened by the examples of Canada and Lebanon, where the existence of fluctuating rates since 1950 and 1948, respectively, did not prevent the authorities from pursuing the most conservative of monetary policies. In December, 1958, Argentina freed the peso rate simultaneously with the adoption of a program of monetary stabilization.

[15] Quoted from J. Viner, "Some International Aspects of Economic Stabilization," in *The State of the Social Sciences*, ed. L. D. White (Chicago: University of Chicago Press, 1956), p. 296. See also L. Robbins, *The Economist in the Twentieth Century* (London: Macmillan, 1954).

[16] This is also Professor Haberler's view. *Currency Convertibility* (Washington: American Enterprise Association, 1954), p. 26.

If a currency has become overvalued as a result of inflation and the authorities decide to apply deflationary measures in order to make possible both the preservation of the given level of exchange rates and the eventual removal of exchange controls, the consequences will be particularly painful. They were demonstrated by the experience of the United Kingdom during the years leading up to the restoration of the pre–World War I gold parity in 1925.[17] It was undoubtedly this trauma more than anything else that prepared the ground for the eventual abandonment of the gold standard. The attempt to preserve an established exchange-rate peg at all costs through harsh deflationary measures (and originally without resorting to strict exchange controls) was exercised once more in Germany at the beginning of the great depression. At the very bottom of the slump, the Reichsbank raised the discount rate from 10 to 15 per cent (August 1, 1931). If we knew more about the subconscious world of economics, we might well find that these policies and their disastrous consequences have been largely responsible for the instinctive refusal of many economists of the generation that witnessed them to recognize central banking as a respectable tool of economic policy.

In a milder form, similar experiences could be observed in a number of countries after World War II. Deflation was in recent years preferred to devaluation of an obviously overvalued currency by countries such as Ireland or Denmark. Perhaps not accidentally, growth rates in these countries have been among the lowest in Europe.[18] More ominously, the same maladjustments are starkly evident in the United States at this time, although the true nature and the seriousness of the trouble seems to be appreciated only by preciously few people.

In a recent article, Professor R. Triffin points out that an excessive rate of credit expansion may under flexible exchange rates entail currency depreciation even though it might initially not cause any disturbances in the cost and price patterns of the country con-

[17] See Keynes's very persuasive essay, "The Economic Consequences of Mr. Churchill," *Essays in Persuasion* (London: Hart-Davis, 1952), pp. 244–70. The British authorities did not peg the rate to begin with but brought the fluctuating rate for the pound sterling toward the target value through monetary policy. We have argued in chapter iv that adjustment ought to be easier under these circumstances than if the rate were rigidly pegged from the very beginning.

[18] See O.E.E.C. Statistical Bulletins, *General Statistics*.

cerned.[19] The depreciation may nevertheless stimulate increases in import prices that could cause irreversible wage and price adjustments. Like Professors Robbins and Viner, Triffin sees a bias toward continuous inflation and a one-way movement of flexible exchange rates, though for slightly different reasons.

This is a persuasive argument against an excessive rate of monetary expansion, but it is less convincing as an argument against exchange-rate flexibility. While overexpansion of credit is likely to cause depreciation under a regime of fluctuating rates, it entails depletion of gold and foreign-exchange reserves when exchange rates are pegged. It is easy similarly to discredit the regime of pegged exchange rates by specifying a rate of credit expansion that would lead to exhaustion of a country's exchange reserves and international drawing rights, no matter how large they may be, even without the adverse speculation that could safely be expected to set in sooner or later. At the same time, one can always specify a rate of credit expansion that avoids depreciation of a flexible rate and, *a fortiori*, any irreversible changes in the price and cost structure that might be induced by it.

The hypothesis that excessive monetary expansion can lead to currency depreciation while prices of domestic products remain stable is unrealistic, particularly under full-employment conditions. Taken literally, this outcome would imply a marginal propensity to spend on imports of unity. The United States has in the past few years experienced a continuous rise in the price level even while the economy was operating considerably *below* the full-employment mark.

It has been shown in chapter ii that adverse speculation tends to induce self-correcting monetary effects when the central bank pegs the exchange rate through stabilizing purchases and sales, whereas these effects are absent under fluctuating rates. Professor Triffin stresses this difference as an additional argument in favor of pegged rates.[20] It seems doubtful, however, whether a central bank that practices unwarranted easy-money policies will feel restrained by this mechanism.

[19] "Tomorrow's Convertibility: Aims and Means of International Monetary Policy," *Banca Nazionale del Lavoro Quarterly Review*, No. 49 (June, 1959), pp. 135–36, reprinted in *Gold and the Dollar Crisis* (New Haven: Yale University Press, 1960), pp. 82–84.

[20] *Banca Nazionale*, p. 138; *Gold and the Dollar Crisis*, pp. 84–85.

W. M. Scammell qualifies his support of flexible exchange rates by sketching a similar sequence of events in which an initial foreign-trade deficit leads to depreciation and ensuing "cost-inflation."[21] He does not specify how the initial deficit is supposed to have developed. If inflationary domestic policies are the cause, it is hardly appropriate to label the subsequent events "cost-inflation," and Scammells' case is identical to Triffin's. If the deficit is due to rising foreign prices of imports, there would be a tendency toward cost inflation even when the exchanges are pegged. Pegged rates are by no means preferable in that case. If the authorities are not prepared to undertake deflationary action, as Scammell generally takes for granted, the cost-price spiral may perhaps develop more slowly, but the deficit will increase more rapidly under pegged rates. The likelihood that trade controls must eventually be imposed is greater. Such controls tend to aggravate the inflationary pressure through progressively more serious misallocation of resources, as emphasized in chapter vi.

The opinion has gained ground in recent years that price stability may conflict with the objective of rapid economic growth.[22] This line of reasoning remains popular in spite of some obvious theoretical deficiencies and lack of support by the available empirical evidence. The advocacy of creeping inflation is usually considered to conflict only with equity considerations, if that much is conceded. Even for a closed economy, however, it should be obvious that inflation, at whatever rate it proceeds, will generally interfere with the efficiency of resource allocation by distorting actual and expected intra- and intertemporal rates of substitution. It could only fail to do this if it were possible for everybody to anticipate the rate of inflation correctly and to hedge against it fully, in which case nominal interest rates and spot and forward prices of all commodities will instantaneously adjust so as to create the same situation in real terms that would have existed if the price level had remained

[21] *International Monetary Policy* (London: Macmillan, 1957), pp. 91–92.

[22] See, e.g., S. S. Slichter, "Thinking Ahead," *Harvard Business Review*, **35** (September–October, 1957), esp. 26, 28; also Professor Slichter's testimony before the Joint Economic Committee of the U.S. Congress, 86th Congress, *Employment, Growth, and Price Levels* (Washington: U.S. Government Printing Office, March, 1959), pp. 2–53; United Nations, *World Economic Survey, 1958* (New York), pp. 1–6.

stable. None of the supposedly stimulating effects of a rising price level can become operative in this case.

Probably even more important is the qualitative deterioration of investment that usually follows from the substitution of direct rationing of credit by banks or by governmental bodies, typical of inflationary conditions, for the rationing by equilibrium interest rates. Misallocation of resources need not necessarily take the form of undue expansion of certain *industries* at the expense of others. It suffices that the weakening of the criterion of investment profitability leads to an expansion both of badly managed and of well-managed firms within the *same* industry, while higher real rates of interest would make more credit available to the latter and allow them to expand at the expense of the former.

Since no economy in the real world is closed, the objections to creeping inflation are even more serious. Many of its advocates seem to be oblivious to the international repercussions of an inflationary trend. In particular, steadily creeping inflation is irreconcilable with pegged exchange rates, although it nevertheless finds many of its supporters among the adherents of the latter. We need not elaborate any further upon the fact that no scheme for increasing international liquidity that presupposes pegged exchange rates and absence of exchange controls can possibly be expected to work as long as some countries consciously promote or passively permit inflation while others preserve—and continue to grow happily with—a highly stable price level.[23] Quite apart from the depletion of reserves, the repercussions of creeping inflation on a country's balance on current account may, when exchange rates are pegged, play havoc with the objective of full employment. Even *if* the claim turned out to be true that the purely *domestic* effects of demand inflation are capable of raising the employment level irrespective of the degree to which labor and commodity markets are infested with imperfections, the responsiveness of demand to changes of relative prices between domestic goods and foreign substitutes may be high enough to cause a net *decrease* of employment.

These issues are illustrated by the present state of the United States balance of payments. The current account has become in-

---

[23] Some empirical evidence on the effect of inflation on the rates of growth of different countries is presented in U Tun Wai, "The Relation between Inflation and Economic Development: A Statistical Inductive Study," *Int. Mon. Fund Staff Papers*, 7 (October, 1959), 302–17.

creasingly less favorable for the United States over the past few years and has even turned into a deficit in 1959, while everybody agreed that the economy was less than fully employed. As long as the unfavorable trend of the balance on goods and services is not reversed, we will be treated to the spectacle of the world's wealthiest country becoming a net borrower from countries whose per capita incomes are in many cases only a small fraction of the United States average. The indifference of a large part of economically sophisticated opinion to the failure of the United States to generate a substantial export surplus, as the world's most highly developed countries have done in the past, and the insistence instead on a further expansion of domestic absorption by an opulent society is disconcerting, to put it mildly.

Professor Triffin has warned of the possible dangers associated with the present practice of central banks of holding certain national currencies as reserves.[24] The parallel with the gold-exchange standard of the 1920's is close, and a repetition of the disorders associated with its breakdown in the early 1930's is a distinct possibility. Internationalization of the world's liquid reserves, as advocated by Professor Triffin, could do much to alleviate these dangers. It would be a mistake, however, to regard such a measure as a substitute for flexible exchange rates (or for the universal adoption of the internal economic policies characteristic of the gold standard). While removing a potential source of trouble in the *capital* accounts of balances of payments, it cannot contribute toward the objective of keeping current accounts in reasonable balance over time or achieving surpluses. As noted above, even the United States is now experiencing difficulties of this kind, while there have as yet been no indications that private and official holders of dollar balances might feel induced to precipitate a flight from the dollar. They may well become concerned, but if so, probably in response to evidence of a further deterioration of the United States balance on goods and services rather than any other cause. Proposals to reorganize international lending institutions would appear to attack the symptoms rather than the cause of the malady.

Apart from its highly successful experiment with fluctuating ex-

---

[24] "The Return to Convertibility: 1926–1931 and 1958——?" *Banca Nazionale del Lavoro Quarterly Review*, No. 48 (March, 1959), pp. 3–57; and "Tomorrow's Convertibility," *ibid.*, No. 49 (June, 1959), pp. 131–200, reprinted in *Gold and the Dollar Crisis*.

change rates, Canada has been an innovator in another respect. In November, 1956, the Bank of Canada adopted a "floating bank rate" by setting its discount rate in any week $\frac{1}{4}$ per cent above the preceding week's tender rate on treasury bills.[25] The implications of this practice deserve more attention than they have received so far. The fact that flexibility of these two important variables has been adopted in the same country is perhaps more than incidental. Our discussion of forward markets has emphasized the intimate connection between the structure of short-term interest rates, on which the bank rate can exercise an obvious influence, and the pattern of exchange rates for various maturities. Considerations involving this relationship apart, essentially the same objections can be raised against the practice of pegging interest rates, or of varying them by discrete jumps, as the ones that apply to pegged exchange rates and to the system of the "adjustable peg." The lack of flexibility is likely to cause maladjustments and disruptive effects on speculative expectations, although these consequences should be less serious in the case of the bank rate, in view of the fact that it is only one, and usually not the most important one, among several short-term interest rates.

3

## CURRENCY OVERVALUATION — AN OBSTACLE TO ECONOMIC GROWTH

A basic dilemma in any underdeveloped country is the cleavage between the needs of vital investment projects and the trickle of domestic resources that is available if the equally vital need to maintain at least the existing standard of living should receive proper attention. Accelerated growth will in most instances be possible only through large-scale foreign investment or aid. If all of a proposed resource deficit is covered by unilateral grants from the rest of the world, no balance-of-payments problem can arise. It is unreasonable to expect that this will ever become the rule rather than the exception. Most of the capital equipment required for rapid economic development will generally have to be provided through private foreign investment. It is only too well known, on the other hand, that the international flow of private capital to those coun-

[25] Bank of Canada, *Annual Report, 1956*, p. 45.

tries that would need it most has, despite a revival in the past few years, been deplorably small.[26]

Several developments are responsible for this state of affairs. The most important factor usually cited is the insecurity of foreign investment occasioned by the risk of default (whether the borrower be a private corporation or a government) or of expropriation. This alone is a convincing explanation for the absence of a large flow of private capital to underdeveloped areas. The establishment of a favorable political and legal climate for foreign investors remains an indispensable condition for a large capital inflow, however understandable may be the lack of sympathy for the cause of foreign absentee capitalists among the populations of underdeveloped countries and their political leaders.

It is evident that exchange-rate policy can under no circumstances be expected to bring about the needed change all by itself. It is perhaps not always sufficiently appreciated that a pegged exchange rate that overvalues a country's currency suffices to inhibit an inflow of private development capital even if no other obstacles stand in its way. Speculative and many forms of long-term capital movements will only be attracted to a country whose currency is expected not to depreciate in the future. If a currency is held at a peg grossly out of line with its true equilibrium value, and if the country's authorities are demonstrably unable or unwilling ever to adopt the harsh deflationary measures that could *make* it the equilibrium rate of exchange—a condition that holds for many underdeveloped countries nowadays—devaluation can only be postponed, never avoided. The acquisition of claims denominated in the currency of such a country does not merely involve an exchange *risk*, as it would with flexible exchanges, but an exchange *loss* known with certainty in advance. The loss could be avoided only if the government guaranteed the reconversion of any capital inflow into the foreigner's currency at the exchange rate at which it came in. Such guarantees are almost universally lacking for bond issues of private business and local governments.

Superficially, direct investment and acquisition of claims denominated in the lender's currency seem to be unaffected by exchange risks. Foreign-exchange difficulties as a result of currency

[26] See the two United Nations publications, *The International Flow of Private Capital, 1946–1952* (New York, 1954); and *The International Flow of Private Capital, 1956–1958* (New York, 1959).

overvaluation must, however, evoke legitimate fears that controls on the repatriation of funds may be imposed. Enough evidence is available to show that this factor decisively influences the magnitude of direct investment. The defense of pegged exchange rates on the grounds that only they can assure a substantial volume of international capital flows involves a delusion *unless* universal faith in the continuity of exchange pegs is maintained by the policies characteristic of the gold-standard era. The system of the "adjustable peg" is more vulnerable on this count than on almost any other. The notion that flexible rates restrain long-term capital movements is persuasively refuted by the fact that Canada has been the world's leading recipient of foreign investment in the 1950's.[27] Even more remarkable is an earlier example. Foreign investment in Argentina reached its highest levels in the years 1885–90, when the Argentine peso was a freely fluctuating currency, even though a galloping inflation was under way at that time.[28]

Governments do not, as a rule, set the exchange rate at an overvalued parity on purpose. It usually becomes overvalued as a result of inflation, after having initially been set in the neighborhood of the true equilibrium value. The urgency of rapid economic growth naturally tempts policymakers in underdeveloped countries to undertake ambitious investment programs. Insufficiently digested Keynesian doctrines often prompt them to apply cheap-money policies with the aim of inducing private industry to a high rate of expansion at the same time that government spending is substantially increased without adequate provisions for a rise in tax revenue.[29] In an underdeveloped country where exuberance rather than a shortage of effective demand is the more serious problem, such policies inevitably give rise to inflation unless the country is able to afford a substantial and continued import surplus provided by foreign investment or free aid. Not only will foreign aid usually not be provided in the required magnitude, but even a slightly in-

[27] International Monetary Fund, *International Financial Statistics;* United Nations, *The International Flow of Private Capital, 1956–1958*, p. 79.

[28] J. H. Williams, *Argentine International Trade under Inconvertible Paper Money, 1880–1900* (Cambridge, Mass.: Harvard University Press, 1920); A. G. Ford, "Flexible Exchange Rates and Argentina, 1885–1900," *Oxford Economic Papers*, Vol. 10 (1958).

[29] The second five-year plan for India (1956–61) may serve as a typical example. Since its inception, a number of modifications have eliminated some of its most objectionable features.

flationary tendency must cut off the bulk of private capital inflow if the exchange rate remains pegged at the old level and the country's currency becomes overvalued as a consequence. The disaster of a precipitous capital *outflow* can be checked by sufficiently stringent controls. But no matter how severe, controls cannot force a capital *inflow*, except for the forcible repatriation of foreign assets held by domestic residents. Apart from this dubious possibility, the mere prevention of capital outflow never provides any additional foreign exchange, and all resources for new development projects have to be squeezed out of the overburdened domestic economy. The mere existence of exchange controls on capital movements often scares off private capital inflow even when the currency is not overvalued. The postwar evidence is very suggestive.[30]

Pegged exchanges are widely held to prevent capital flight that might take place when the exchange rate is flexible. But it should be obvious that the inducement to move out funds is stronger, not weaker, when foreign exchange is kept artificially cheap. It is not the constancy of an artificially pegged exchange rate, but only *exchange controls* that can prevent the outflow of capital. As long as the authorities are willing to resort to exchange controls, capital flight can be checked under flexible rates not only equally well but even better, since the appreciation of foreign currency under the impact of inflation partially removes the incentive to move funds abroad.[31]

We should not jump to the conclusion that inflation does not matter if a country adopts fluctuating exchange rates. As long as an inflationary trend is expected to continue, the public will anticipate further depreciation. Speculative as well as most other types of capital inflow may be discouraged too much for comfort, whether exchange rates are pegged or flexible. The maintenance of monetary stability is likely to be an indispensable prerequisite for extensive participation of foreign capital in a country's economic development, no matter what regime of exchange-rate management is adopted.

[30] Cf. Triffin, *Europe and the Money Muddle*, p. 236.

[31] It is true that the existence of trade restrictions for balance-of-payments purposes is, almost by definition, incompatible with freely fluctuating rates in the true sense of the word. The absence of exchange controls has, in fact, been made an integral part of our definition of flexible rates. This definitional difficulty in no way weakens our contention that pegged rates have often taken the credit for the dubious achievements of exchange controls.

Proponents of pegged exchange rates have usually had in mind a further consequence of capital flight when exchanges are flexible. Depreciation of domestic currency in the wake of inflation is believed to add more fuel to the inflationary fire by increasing the cost of imports as well as the inducement to export. Again, this may be an argument for the prevention of capital outflow by strict exchange controls, but not for pegged exchanges. What really matters is the availability and the allocation of resources once a certain level of money national income is given. When capital inflow is discouraged by the prospect of substantial depreciation in the future (whether the exchange rate is pegged or flexible) while all speculative capital outflow is prevented by exchange controls, a country deprives itself equally effectively of the voluntary supply of foreign resources by investors from abroad, however successful it may be in plugging all possible leaks. In the short run, an addition to the availability of foreign resources is possible through depletion of the exchange reserves held by the monetary authorities. Central banks or exchange stabilization boards are able to exhaust their reserves of foreign exchange with equal facility when exchange rates are free to move and when they are pegged, however.

At first glance, we conclude that the acceleration of an existing inflationary trend by international capital movements (or by their absence) is the same whether exchange rates are pegged or flexible, assuming equal severity of exchange controls. In view of the principal argument of chapter vi, flexible exchange rates appear in a more favorable light even in this respect. Depreciation of a flexible rate makes it possible to maintain exports that would be cut off under pegged rates as the inflation continues, and international trade is not prevented from continuing in the channels dictated by comparative advantage. To the extent that this makes it possible to avoid a reduction in the country's real income according to the usual index-number criteria, currency depreciation under inflationary conditions serves to *dampen* the upward movement of prices.

4

## POLICY RECOMMENDATIONS

Whichever aspect we consider, it is clear that the claims usually made for pegged exchanges are partly attributable to the exchange controls often associated with them, and for the rest are valid if the pegging of rates is combined with strong and flexible monetary and fiscal policies to make the pegged rate the actual equilibrium rate at all times, or to keep it sufficiently close to it so that temporary balance-of-payments disequilibria can be bridged by the available foreign-exchange reserves. Only then will it be possible to do without exchange controls or close substitutes in the form of other quantitative restrictions, and only then do foreign investors have the assurance that currency parities will not be changed. *If* these exacting standards of public policy were always assured, little could be said against pegged exchange rates except that they cripple one of the most promising mechanisms for effective monetary policy. This alone is a rather formidable objection. No more need be said about this aspect of exchange-rate management; it has received detailed treatment in chapter iv above.

We have built up a case against the administrative pegging of exchange rates at arbitrary levels and the subsequent adjustment of other economic variables to that level by brute force. An at least equally convincing case has emerged, on the other hand, for strong monetary policies designed to promote price stability and (given identical policies in other countries) to guarantee a high degree of stability for flexible exchange rates in this way rather than through direct intervention on the foreign-exchange markets. As far as supporters of pegged rates have had the aim of reasonable exchange-rate stability over the long run in mind, there remains little room for disagreement on basic objectives. The analysis presented in earlier chapters should have made it amply clear, however, that the differences between rigid pegging and monetary policies designed to promote long-run stability of a flexible rate are absolutely fundamental.

We have already touched on the question of what the appropriate role of government intervention in the foreign-exchange markets ought to be. It has been made clear that, ideally, competitive speculation with free entry guarantees a maximum of stability, provided that speculators assess future exchange-rate movements correctly. These conditions will not necessarily be fulfilled all the time. The basic rules for governments to follow are, first of all, to create an environment in which high accuracy of foresight is assured and, second, to pattern any intervention in the foreign-exchange markets so as to create the results which well-informed, perfectly competitive speculation would ideally bring about.

[ 135 ]

Milton Friedman has argued that a simple criterion is available to judge the success of a government stabilization board: the profitability of its operations.[32] It is evident, however, that Pareto-optimality which Professor Friedman so clearly advocates elsewhere requires the mimicking of perfect competition in this field as well and, hence, zero profits for the stabilization agency over the long run.

For a time after exchange rates are set free it may be necessary for the government to undertake stabilizing action until the public has become accustomed to the system and speculation performs its functions properly. Hard and fast rules for the proper degree of intervention are difficult to give in the abstract. It should be possible for central bankers to develop a feeling for the dose that is just sufficient to smooth out irritable oscillations without going against the trend of the market, just as they have learned to tell the difference between open-market operations and the act of pegging interest rates on government bonds. I share the view of many supporters of flexible exchanges that the best solution in the long run is for the authorities to remain almost completely aloof from the exchange markets.[33] In chapter iv we have argued, moreover, that whatever intervention is undertaken should best be confined to forward markets. One of the many advantages of exclusive reliance on the forward market as an adjustment tool would be the elimination of the need for central banks or associated agencies of carrying an inventory of foreign-exchange reserves. The problem of "international liquidity" which has been discussed so frequently in recent years

[32] *Essays*, p. 188.

An article by H. C. Eastman and S. Stykolt, "Exchange Stabilization in Canada, 1950–54," *Canadian Journal of Economics and Political Science*, 22 (1956), 221–33, gives the erroneous impression that a stabilization agency should attempt not only to make money but to *maximize* profits. See also the more guarded "Exchange Stabilization Further Considered" by the same authors and the "Comment" by C. P. Kindleberger, *Canadian Journal*, 23 (1957), 404–8. The discussion was continued with a "Comment" by P. Wonnacott and a reply by Eastman and Stykolt, *Canadian Journal*, 24 (May, 1958), 262–72.

[33] Professor Meade has argued that there is always the danger that the exchange stabilization funds of different countries might work at cross-purposes in a multilateral system of flexible exchange rates. He points out that it might prove desirable to leave any intervention that remains to be done to an international stabilization agency. J. E. Meade, "The Case for Variable Exchange Rates," *Three Banks Review*, September, 1955; also *The Balance of Payments*, p. 226.

would be solved with one stroke.[34] At the same time, the absence of large deposits by central banks in "reserve centers" eliminates the danger that these deposits might be withdrawn all of a sudden whenever a reserve currency is expected to depreciate.

The attitude of many economists and bankers toward proposals to intervene on the forward exchange markets reveals a lack of understanding of some of the basic functions of exchange markets. Many adherents to the principle of pegged (spot) exchange rates nevertheless favor freely fluctuating forward rates on the grounds that bear speculation against a currency by forward sales should be penalized as much as possible while commercial exporters and importers are relieved of exchange risks. This has been official British policy during the past few years. P. Einzig reports that during the 1920's and 1930's the Netherlands Bank also followed a deliberate policy of causing forward depreciation of the Dutch guilder on several occasions.[35] Apart from the fact that such a policy accentuates the loss of reserves through interest arbitrage, as stressed by Einzig and recently again by Jasay and Spraos,[36] its proponents also forget that many, if not most, exporters and importers *qua* nonspeculative commercial traders ought to depend on *forward* exchange rates rather than spot.[37] To the extent that freedom from exchange risk for regular commercial trade is a desirable objective, this policy consequently aims at pegging that exchange rate whose stability is least important for it. Central banks have occasionally intervened in forward markets in the appropriate direction, al-

[34] The International Monetary Fund has prepared two memoranda on the topic, "The Adequacy of Monetary Reserves," *Int. Mon. Fund Staff Papers*, 3 (1953), 181–227, and *International Reserves and Liquidity* (Washington: International Monetary Fund, August, 1958). See also the two recent articles by Triffin cited in n. 24 above, "The Return to Convertibility: 1926–1931 and 1958——?" and "Tomorrow's Convertibility," reprinted in *Gold and the Dollar Crisis*. A more idiosyncratic proposal for increasing international liquidity is a rise in the dollar price of gold. It recurs as a *ceterum censeo* in many of Sir Roy Harrod's recent writings. Cf. *The Pound Sterling, 1951–1958* ("Essays in International Finance," No. 30 [Princeton: Princeton University Press, 1958]), p. 17.

[35] *The Theory of Forward Exchange* (London: Macmillan, 1937), pp. 375–77.

[36] *Ibid.*; A. E. Jasay, "Making Currency Reserves 'Go Round,'" *Journal of Political Economy*, 66 (1958), 353–56; J. Spraos, "Speculation, Arbitrage and Sterling," *Economic Journal*, 69 (1959), 1–21; and the discussion on "Exchange Policy in the Forward Market" by Jasay, Spraos, and anon., *The Banker*, Vol. 108 (April, 1958).

[37] See chap. iv, sec. 2 above.

though the instances in which this is known to have happened are extremely few.[38] By and large, bankers have seen forward markets primarily as a vehicle for speculation whose use should be discouraged by all possible means.[39]

For those who adhere to the principle of pegged exchange rates, the refusal to intervene on the forward markets is irrational also with regard to its psychological effects. The public will necessarily interpret unwillingness to defend the forward rate against a bear attack as an admission that the monetary authorities themselves do not believe in the continuity of what they profess to stabilize. Bear speculators can under these circumstances hardly be accused of "undermining confidence in the currency" by "destabilizing" operations. Whenever the central bank is earnestly devoted to the preservation of an established peg, its unwillingness to intervene on forward markets also neglects a profitable business opportunity, as well as its proclaimed objective of safeguarding the stability of those exchange rates that count most for regular commercial trade.

It should hardly be necessary at this stage to emphasize again the paramount importance of freedom of capital movements for the smooth functioning of the system. Effective speculation and arbitrage, the vital lubricants for smoothing out the innumerable short-run rigidities present in the real world, are impossible if capital movements are prohibited or if they are subject to time-consuming official scrutiny.[40] Wherever governments have not completely renounced central banking as a policy tool, speculation has revealed itself as a genuine stabilizer. Canada's success with exchange flexibility since 1950 has, in this as well as other respects, frequently baffled even the optimists. The essentially theoretical nature of this study precluded a detailed appraisal of empirical data. It is only fitting to re-

[38] See Einzig, *The Theory of Forward Exchange*, chaps. xxxvi and xxxviii.

[39] During a meeting of central bankers in 1931, the representative of the German Reichsbank stated his view that "every forward market has strongly speculative tendencies. By participating in forward transactions, [we] would be recognizing that such speculative factors have a justification to which they are not properly entitled." Quoted by Einzig, *The Theory of Forward Exchange*, p. 327. See also Keynes's scathing remarks in "The Future of the Foreign Exchanges," *Lloyds Bank Monthly Review*, December, 1935.

[40] For a statement of the opposite view, held by the majority of economists during the first postwar decade, see R. Nurkse, "Conditions of International Monetary Equilibrium," reprinted in *Readings in the Theory of International Trade*, pp. 8, 13.

mark, however, that one could hardly hope for a more persuasive empirical verification of the conclusions of this monograph than the one the Canadian experiment provides. In none of the other countries in which fluctuating exchange rates have been adopted since World War II does the evidence lend any support to the fears expressed by their opponents.[41] We cannot hope to convince those who seem to argue that, as Abba P. Lerner once aptly put it, "Even if it happened, it couldn't." But for the rest of us, a proposition reportedly formulated by Kenneth E. Boulding will do: "What is, is possible."

[41] The Canadian experience is evaluated in R. R. Rhomberg's recent doctoral dissertation, "Fluctuating Exchange Rates in Canada: Short-term Capital Movements and Domestic Stability," Yale University, 1959, summarized in "Canada's Foreign Exchange Market," *Int. Mon. Fund Staff Papers*, 7 (1960), 439–56. For the interwar period, some of the misleading conclusions in the late Ragnar Nurkse's League of Nations study, *International Currency Experience* (New York: Columbia University Press, 1944), have been corrected in Tsiang's "Fluctuating Exchange Rates in Countries with Relatively Stable Economies," pp. 244–73. Lebanon's experience since 1948 has yet to attract the attention it deserves. Unlike Canada, Lebanon has not abrogated the official par value of its currency, in an apparently successful effort not to incur the wrath of the International Monetary Fund. No transactions have been taking place at the par value since 1952. I am indebted to J. M. Montias for having called my attention to the Lebanese experiment. More evidence will become available in Argentina, where exchange rates were set free in December, 1958.

# APPENDIX

## *Welfare Aspects of International Trade*

We have repeatedly used arguments that rested on welfare considerations, without giving the latter more than a very cursory treatment in the main body of the text. For readers with little prior knowledge of welfare economics, this appendix will develop a few of the ideas most relevant to the topics discussed in this study. We shall restrict ourselves to the barest fundamentals. No interpersonal comparisons are assumed, nor shall we discuss external economies or diseconomies, among other things.[1]

### 1

#### GEOMETRY

The condition for a welfare optimum that the marginal rate of transformation between two commodities should equal the marginal rate of substitution in consumption for all individuals can be illustrated for the two-person, two-commodity case by means of a simple graphical device.

Let $PQ$ in Figure 8 be the usual transformation curve (or production block) between commodities $X$ and $Y$, derived from the underlying production functions under the assumption of constant fac-

---

[1] The principal literature references for this Appendix will be two articles by R. E. Baldwin, "Equilibrium in International Trade: A Diagrammatical Analysis" and "The New Welfare Economics and Gains in International Trade," *Quarterly Journal of Economics*, 62 (1948), 748–62 and 66 (1952), 91–101, respectively; J. de V. Graaff, "On Optimum Tariff Structures," *Review of Economic Studies*, 17 (1949–50), 47–59; P. A. Samuelson, "Evaluation of Real National Income," *Oxford Economic Papers*, N.S., 2 (1950), 1–29; and P. B. Kenen, "On the Geometry of Welfare Economics," *Quarterly Journal of Economics*, 71 (1957), 426–47.

tor supplies and perfect competition in the factor markets. Also given are the indifference maps of two consumers $A$ and $B$. An arbitrarily selected indifference curve of the first individual, $I_A$, is superimposed on the graph of the transformation curve. Holding the first consumer at the utility level indicated by $I_A$, we want to find the second individual's most preferred position. The indifference map of consumer $B$ is moved across the diagram in such a way that its origin $O_B$ always rests on $I_A$. If all relevant loci have the usual curvature, there will be one, and only one, point $O'_B$ for which the

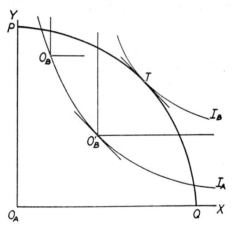

FIG. 8.—Optimal resource allocation under autarky in the case of two commodities and two individuals. $T$ indicates the total quantities produced, $O'_B$ the quantities consumed by individual $A$.

transformation locus touches the highest indifference curve of consumer $B$. This curve is denoted by $I_B$. The point of tangency, $T$, indicates the point of optimum production under the given constraints (maximum utility for consumer $B$ for a given utility level of $A$).

The diagram shows at the same time the optimal allocation of the total quantities of $X$ and $Y$ among the two individuals for the fixed utility level of consumer $A$. The two consumers should receive the quantities indicated by the co-ordinates of $O'_B$ with respect to $O_A$ (for individual $A$) and the co-ordinates of $T$ with respect to $O'_B$ (for individual $B$). Optimality of this particular division of total output requires that the slopes of the relevant indifference curves $I_A$ and $I_B$ at the points $O'_B$ and $T$ be equal. Let us assume that the proposition

[ 142 ]

were untrue and that the slopes of $I_A$ and $I_B$ at the points $O'_B$ and $T$ could differ, as in Figure 9. We move the indifference map of consumer $B$ downward a little farther, with its origin sliding along $I_A$. In the immediate neighborhood of $O'_B$, the movement of the origin along $I_A$ coincides with a movement along the tangent $t''$. The point $T$ on the (by hypothesis) highest attainable indifference curve $I_B$ of individual $B$ moves along the line $t'$, which is parallel to $t''$. But $I_B$ must now intersect the transformation locus and cannot have been $B$'s highest attainable indifference curve.[2]

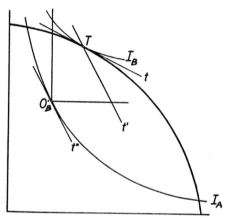

Fig. 9.—Non-optimal resource allocation under autarky

The procedure is easily generalized for any number of individuals. Consider $N$ consumers $A$, $B$, . . . $N$ in a perfectly competitive model economy producing two commodities $X$ and $Y$. Each individual is equipped with a certain budget and confronted with equilibrium money prices of the two commodities. Production is indicated by the point $T$ on the transformation locus whose slope

[2] It need hardly be stressed that the uniqueness of the optimum position is only due to the fact that we have specified a constant utility level for one of the individuals. Starting from a different indifference curve of consumer $A$, we would in general expect to land at a different "optimum" point on the transformation locus, unless the two individuals have identical tastes and all income-consumption curves are straight lines through the origin. On the other hand, a reversal of our procedure in the sense of holding $B$'s utility level constant at $I_B$ and then finding $A$'s most preferred position will lead us to the same point on the transformation curve and an identical distribution of the two commodities.

[ 143 ]

equals the existing price ratio (Fig. 10). We draw the budget line and the highest attainable indifference curve $I_A$ of consumer $A$ through $T$ and infer the origin $O_A$ of his indifference map from his budget and the given prices. The budget line and the highest attainable indifference curve $I_B$ of individual $B$ are now drawn through $O_A$. Their slope at $O_A$ is, in general equilibrium, equal to the slope of $I_A$ at $T$. Again, we find the origin $O_B$ and continue in the same fashion up to the $N$th consumer. Equilibrium requires that $O_N$ co-

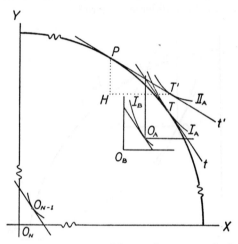

Fig. 10.—Potential superiority of free trade over autarky in the two-commodity, $n$-individual case.

incide with the origin of the production transformation curve. Convexity of the indifference curves of all $N$ individuals in the neighborhood of their observed consumption points, as required for stability, implies that any movement along the transformation locus away from $T$ must lower the utility level of at least one consumer.

2

APPLICATION TO INTERNATIONAL TRADE

Assume that the economy is opened and that residents can trade at the world price ratio $t'$. This permits situations such as the one depicted in Figure 10, with production at $P$ and consumption at $T'$, exports of $Y$ equal to $PH$, and imports of $X$ equal to $HT'$. But consumption at $T'$ instead of $T$ allows consumer $A$ to move to a higher indifference curve $II_A$ while the consumption (and hence the utility) levels of all other individuals can be held constant (the origins of all indifference maps, $O_A$, $O_B$, ... $O_N$ may remain fixed). The feasibility of improvements of this kind shows that the introduction of trade leads to an unambiguous increase in *potential* welfare. This demonstration of the familiar doctrine of comparative advantage is, it will be noted, built entirely on individual indifference maps and nowhere requires the use of any one of the variety of community indifference curves.

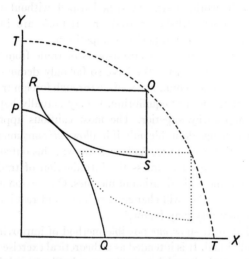

FIG. 11.—Derivation of the optimal world production locus from the production blocks of two countries.

The Pareto-optimality of free trade for a world of two countries can be shown by a simple extension of our construction. In Figure 11, the production transformation curve of another country, *RS*, has been rotated 180 degrees and moved across the co-ordinate system in such a way that the two production blocks always touch each other. The origin of the production block of the second country will trace out a locus of optimal production points for the world as a whole, *TT*. If perfect competition rules within each country's economy, no internal reallocation of given factor supplies will make it possible to transcend the optimal world transformation locus.[3]

[3] A construction of this kind was first used in A. P. Lerner's "The Diagrammatical Representation of Cost Conditions in International Trade," reprinted from *Economica* (1932) in his *Essays in Economic Analysis* (London: Macmillan 1953), pp. 85–100.

The production pattern brought about by perfect competition within each country insures tangency of the two production blocks only when relative prices are the same in both countries (apart from differences owing to transport costs). This condition will, in turn, generally require unobstructed freedom of commodity movements. Whenever international trade is impeded and, as a result, relative commodity prices diverge, total world production must fall short of the optimal production locus. We can deduce that at least one individual in the world at large must be harmed, without any improvement for others, whenever trade restrictions are imposed in a regime of free trade and perfect competition.

Let us return to the welfare aspects of trade from the point of view of a single country. We have so far only demonstrated a *potential* increase in community welfare through foreign trade, without claiming that the new equilibrium it may actually happen to produce is necessarily superior. The most cautious approach would consider a change desirable only if it allows *all* consumers to land on higher indifference curves. As is well known, this outcome can generally not be expected unless the introduction of trade is accompanied by some redistribution of incomes. One reason among many is that factor wages will change; a reduction of real income of part of the community may follow.[4]

We shall next show *one* possible method of improving the lot of every individual. It is intended as a theoretical exercise without any claim to practical usefulness. The case is illustrated for two consumers, $A$ and $N$; the extension of the argument to any number of individuals is obvious.

In Figure 12, equilibrium before trade is indicated by $T$. Trade is opened up and the country finds itself confronted with a world price ratio $t'$. In order to let each individual benefit from the introduction of trade, we may observe his actual consumption before trade and introduce a system of taxes and subsidies which gives everybody exactly the money income that would allow him to consume, at the post-trade prices, the commodity bundle he used to purchase in the pre-trade equilibrium.

Such a scheme is always feasible. It will, in fact, always result in

[4] W. F. Stolper and P. A. Samuelson, "Protection and Real Wages," *Review of Economic Studies*, Vol. 9 (1941), reprinted in American Economic Association, *Readings in the Theory of International Trade* (Philadelphia: Blakiston, 1950) pp. 333–57.

a profit for the administering authority unless the transformation locus has a kink at the autarky point. For the two consumers in Figure 12, the suggested compensation scheme would involve taxes and subsidies so that the new budget lines coincide with $u'$ and $u''$. Production moves to $P$. Individual $N$ will change his consumption from $O_A$ to $O'_A$, increasing his indifference level from $I_N$ to $II_N$. Let $A$'s indifference map undergo a parallel displacement to the new origin $O'_A$. His old consumption point $T$ is now located at $T'$. The adjustment in his budget allows him to move to $C'$, increasing his

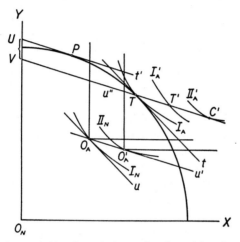

FIG. 12.—A tax-subsidy scheme for improving the position of every individual in a move from autarky to free trade.

utility level from $I'_A$ to $II'_A$. The authorities have at their disposal a surplus equal to the value of $UV$ units of commodity $Y$. This illustrates the possibility of "overcompensation" after the introduction of foreign trade, as discussed by Hicks, Kaldor, Little, Samuelson, Scitovsky, and others.[5]

[5] It is not suggested that governments in the real world should indeed act according to this prescription. Administrative difficulties, political obstacles, or a belief that equity is better served when no income redistribution is effected after the introduction of trade may render its execution unfeasible or undesirable. Nevertheless, there is merit in spelling out policy recommendations with operational significance in the sense that they could conceivably be carried out and would have exactly predictable consequences under ideal conditions. Since the recommendations outlined here do not require interpersonal welfare comparisons, they would entail an unambiguous improvement according to anybody's welfare function except that of a "social masochist."

[ 147 ]

Whereas free trade unambiguously raises the potential welfare level as compared to *autarky*, it is well known that it is not necessarily the best possible situation from the point of view of a single country's egotistic interest, even after a suitable redistribution of incomes. Whenever foreign demand is less than infinitely elastic, the imposition of restrictions improves the terms of trade. Up to a point, the country will gain from the exploitation of its monopoly power. A "gain" is defined, as before, as the feasibility of raising one or more individuals to a higher indifference level without harming others. It follows from continuity considerations that, starting from given indifference levels for all individuals and holding all utility levels but one constant, a certain degree of trade restriction must lead the favored individual to the highest attainable indifference level somewhere between free trade and autarky. The "optimum" tariff or quota is higher the lower is the elasticity of foreign reciprocal demand.[6]

This is as far as we can legitimately go without introducing interpersonal comparisons. The term "optimum tariff" is misleading, since it gives an impression of uniqueness that is quite inappropriate. Unless highly unrealistic homogeneity postulates are imposed on individual indifference maps, the "optimum" trade restriction will generally differ for every conceivable income distribution in the community.[7]

[6] It seems that Auspitz and Lieben have to be credited with the earliest precise statement in print of the optimum-tariff argument (*Untersuchungen über die Theorie des Preises* [Leipzig: Duncker and Humblot, 1889], pp. 415–18 and Figs. 73, 74). The argument is carried surprisingly far. The authors are aware of the symmetry between import and export duties, for example (p. 418). Apart from Viner (*Studies in the Theory of International Trade* [New York: Harper, 1937], pp. 592–93), their contribution is never mentioned in the literature of today, although it was acknowledged by Edgeworth ("The Theory of International Values," *Economic Journal*, 4 [1894], 636).

For later rediscoveries and refinements, see T. de Scitovsky, "A Reconsideration of the Theory of Tariffs," *Review of Economic Studies*, Vol. 9 (1941–42), reprinted in the American Economic Association's *Readings in the Theory of International Trade*, pp. 358–89; S. S. Alexander's "Devaluation versus Import Restriction as an Instrument for Improving Foreign Balance," *International Monetary Fund Staff Papers*, Vol. 1 (1950–51), and J. M. Fleming's "On Making the Best of Balance of Payments Restrictions on Imports," *Economic Journal*, 61 (1951), 48–71; J. de V. Graaff, "On Optimum Tariff Structures."

[7] The only treatments of the terms-of-trade argument in which this qualification is taken into account are Graaff's and Kenen's papers mentioned in n. 1 above. The reader is referred to these articles for further details; we shall not pursue the matter here.

It is also worth noting that (limited) controls will necessarily lead to a potential improvement for a single country only if perfect competition rules in its internal economy. The exposure of previously sheltered domestic monopolies or oligopolies to competition from abroad may otherwise lead to an improvement in resource allocation that outweighs any possible losses through deterioration of the country's terms of trade. The smaller the country, the more important will be this aspect of freer trade, which is quite independent of considerations concerning comparative advantage. Intensification of internal competition following the gradual liberalization of trade is probably one of the principal causes of the rapid growth of European economies in recent years.[8]

## 3

### WELFARE IMPLICATIONS OF INDEX NUMBERS[9]

In previous sections, the potential superiority of free trade to autarky was demonstrated by pointing out that free trade provides an opportunity for some members of the community to attain higher utility levels without sacrifices by others. Although it was established that positions existed along the offer curve of the rest of the world for which this was true, we were not concerned with the question which one of these positions, if any, would actually be realized. In Professor Samuelson's language, free trade is preferable to autarky in a "situation" sense,[10] i.e., it provides the community with a locus of choices of which certain points are found to offer a potential welfare improvement over autarky. Index-number criteria, on the other hand, do not compare *situations* in the sense defined above, but specific *points* in the commodity space. The question arises whether it is possible also to attach welfare significance to comparisons between single points. In chapter vi, use is made of two index-number inequalities to define an "unambiguous increase

[8] This factor has received special emphasis in T. de Scitovsky's *Economic Theory and Western European Integration* (Stanford: Stanford University Press, 1958).

[9] The basic reference for this section will be P. A. Samuelson's "Evaluation of Real National Income," *Oxford Economic Papers*, N.S., 2 (1950), 1–29.

I am indebted to Robert E. Baldwin for having pointed out ambiguities in my article "The Effect of Devaluation on the Price Level," *Quarterly Journal of Economics*, 72 (1958), 273–83, where some of these issues were also discussed.

[10] *Ibid.*, p. 12.

in real income." We shall now investigate the welfare implications of this criterion.

In ordinary language, the inequalities (1) $\Sigma P_2 Q_2 \geqq \Sigma P_2 Q_1$ and (2) $\Sigma P_1 Q_2 > \Sigma P_1 Q_1$ say that the output of goods produced in period 2 has a higher value than (according to the first inequality, possibly the same value as) the output of period 1, whether the quantities are weighted by the prices of the first or those of the second period. Figure 10 illustrates the fulfilment of the two inequalities if the points $T$ and $T'$ indicate the levels of output of periods 1 and 2.

If we were dealing with a single rational individual, the first condition is all we would need to ascertain that position 2 is preferred to position 1. The second inequality is already implied by the first. For a community of individuals, on the other hand, both inequalities together convey less information than the first one does for a single individual. What condition (1) indicates in this case is that, *provided competitive exchange equilibrium holds in position 2, the total quantities of commodities available in point 1 cannot be redistributed in any way that would leave everybody better off than in point 2.*[11]

Samuelson's geometric demonstration of the condition for the case of two individuals and two commodities is reproduced in Figure 13.[12] It may be helpful to draw Figure 13 on two sheets of transparent paper. All the points and the solidly drawn lines should go on the lower sheet, the broken lines on the upper. The lower left-hand corner denotes the origin of the indifference map of the first individual. Point 2 is the upper right-hand corner of an Edgeworth-Bowley box indicating the total quantities available in position 2. It also indicates the origin of the indifference map of the second individual, rotated 180 degrees. The point of tangency inside the box, $T$, shows the actual distribution of the commodities in position 2. The indifference curves of the two individuals through that point are also drawn.

By sliding the upper sheet across the lower one, point 2 on the upper sheet will trace out the upper corners of Edgeworth-Bowley boxes of different sizes. Through the original position of point 2, a line has been drawn with the slope given by the price ratio of position 2. This line divides the commodity space into two halves.

[11] This was first stated by J. R. Hicks in "The Valuation of the Social Income," *Economica*, N.S., 7 (1940), 111.

[12] "Evaluation of Real National Income," p. 8, n. 1.

Inequality (1) holds for all points in the lower half, such as *1*, and for points along the line through point *2*, such as *1'*. It can easily be verified by sliding the two transparent sheets against each other that the commodity totals of none of the points in the lower half-space suffice to realize higher utility levels for *both* individuals than the ones they actually reach in position 2. This proves the Hicks theorem stated above in italics. Only points in the shaded area northeast of the Scitovsky-type community indifference curve through point *2* are superior to *2* in the sense used here. This curve

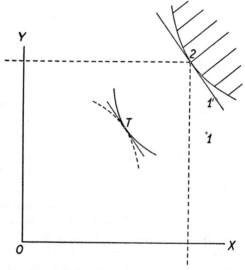

Fɪɢ. 13.—Illustration of the welfare aspects of index numbers

is traced out by point *2* when the upper sheet is slid in such a way that the indifference curves attained by the two individuals in position 2 always touch. In contemplating a move from any point *1* to any point *2*, inequality (1) is thus revealed to be a *sufficient* condition for the fulfilment of Scitovsky's second criterion, that we "must make sure that the people who are against the change would be incapable of bribing those in favor to vote against it, without thereby losing more than they would if the change were carried."[13]

By a mere change of subscripts, it is also seen that the inequality $\Sigma P_1 Q_2 \leqq \Sigma P_1 Q_1$ would imply that no redistribution of the com-

[13] T. de Scitovsky, "A Reconsideration of the Theory of Tariffs," reprinted in *Readings in the Theory of International Trade*, p. 362.

modity totals of point *2* can make every individual better off than he is in point *1*, given competitive exchange equilibrium in the latter. The reverse inequality, (2) $\Sigma P_1 Q_2 > \Sigma P_1 Q_1$, is therefore a *necessary* condition for the fulfilment of Scitovsky's first requirement for an improvement in potential welfare (also known as the "Kaldor-Hicks criterion"): "We must . . . see whether the people benefited by the change could fully compensate those prejudiced by it and still be better off than they were before the change."[14]

To summarize, condition (1) is sufficient but not necessary, whereas condition (2) is necessary but not sufficient for a welfare improvement according to the corresponding Scitovsky criteria. Inequality (1) fails to isolate part of the positions that are inferior to point *2*. These are the points in the region between the price line and the Scitovsky community indifference curve through *2* in Figure 13. Similarly, there is a region that is worse than point *1*, according to the Kaldor-Hicks-Scitovsky definition, without being revealed as such by inequality (2). The index-number inequalities are not exact indicators of potential welfare for finite changes.

For several reasons, it is nevertheless questionable whether the merciless pounding at index-number criteria by economic theorists is justified. First of all, the index-number inequalities coincide with the Scitovsky criteria for infinitesimally small changes. The relative "welfare content" of points in the commodity space is registered more sharply the smaller is the given change. Second, even the correct Scitovsky criteria indicate only changes in *potential* welfare. Economic policy measures are hardly ever such that everybody is made better off, even though this might be potentially feasible. The double Scitovsky criterion and the index-number comparisons are equally vulnerable on this count. On the other hand, modern welfare states usually insure that measures of economic policy do not redistribute incomes too violently. This implies not only an increased likelihood that changes for which a *potential* improvement is indicated will also carry with them an *actual* improvement for the vast majority but also that misjudgments owing to the inherent inaccuracy of the double index-number comparison are less likely to be important.

The reasons are easily seen. The index-number criterion is indeterminate in any case unless both inequalities point in the same direction. Let us assume that both indicate higher real income in

[14] *Ibid.*

position 2. Inequality (1) errs on the side of conservatism if position 1 is the point of departure. Mistakes due to index-number inaccuracy can in this case occur only if inequality (2) indicates superiority of position 2, whereas the correct Scitovsky criterion would reveal 1 to be better than 2. But this combination of circumstances would require that the Scitovsky-type community indifference curve through *1* pass above point *2* while the price line through point *2* (with a slope corresponding to the prices ruling in position 2) passes above point *1*. This constellation presupposes a fairly drastic redistribution of incomes.

The last reason for the acceptance of the double index-number criterion as a reasonable indicator of welfare changes is the least defensible and at the same time the most persuasive one: index numbers are the *only* indicators available in practice unless one is prepared to enter the metaphysical terrain of welfare functions. Even if one wanted to avoid interpersonal comparisons of utility, the application of the double Scitovsky criterion presupposes knowledge of the indifference surfaces of all individuals in a community, an Orwellian vision.

The question to be answered next concerns the index-number changes that can be expected from adjustments in a country's foreign trade.

The movement from autarky to free trade must necessarily result in a rise in real income in terms of the two index-number inequalities *unless* Giffen's paradox holds for imports. This is seen by inspection of Figure 10. The fulfilment of inequality (1) is immediately evident (perfect elasticity of foreign demand, which we had assumed in Figure 10, is not necessary). At first sight, one might think that nothing definite can be said about inequality (2). This doubt is dispelled if one remembers that the relative price of imports falls after the opening of trade and that domestic residents must buy a larger quantity of imports when trade is free unless imports are Giffen goods. It follows that the consumption point realized after trade must lie above and to the right of the price line through the point of autarky. The possibility of a fall in the consumption of the export good does not matter. Giffen's paradox, it will be noted, is not even *sufficient* to insure a reversal of our conclusion.

Ambiguity may arise for smaller movements in the region between the extremes of autarky and free trade. If foreign demand is perfectly elastic and Giffen's paradox does not hold for imports, however, even a partial movement toward freer trade must, for the reasons just stated, produce an increase in real income according to both index-number inequalities. Less-than-perfect elasticity of the foreign offer curve makes the free-trade position less than optimal. Restrictions on foreign trade will then raise a country's potential welfare level, and this may or may not be reflected by the two index-number criteria if positions with trade restrictions are compared with the free-trade point.

The search for the *optimal* degree of trade restriction should not be taken to be more than a pedagogically useful exercise. This monograph has attempted to develop theoretical results that have meaning and significance for economic policy. Propositions involving the "optimum tariff" concept require that policymakers know the shape of all individual indifference surfaces and are able to apply a welfare function to them. These assumptions are plainly inadmissible in any discussion of problems relevant in the real world.

We have entirely avoided social indifference maps. Occasional references to single community indifference curves of the Scitovsky type do not constitute an exception. All propositions based on them could have been traced back to the indifference curves of single individuals from which they were derived. Since there is no proposition in welfare economics, short of interpersonal comparisons, which could not be derived by the use of individual indifference maps, there is no convincing reason why community indifference maps should ever be used for many of the purposes to which they have been applied. It may be thought that they are indispensable for analyzing the comparative-static effects of alternative commercial policies or changes in behavioral parameters on the volume, relative prices, and composition of trade. As in the revealed-preference approach to demand analysis in the case of a single individual, we could imagine that we confront the community with a number of prices for the two commodities and record the positions it "chooses." It may be that, under ideal conditions and in a sufficiently small neighborhood, these points could be assembled into an offer curve which gives the appearance of coming from an indifference map with all the regular properties. No welfare connotations whatsoever can, however, be associated with such a "community behavior map." This remains true even if we follow the empirically unjustifiable assumption, sometimes made for convenience, that the community consists of identical individuals with homothetic indifference curves (i.e., with income-consumption curves that are straight lines through the origin) *unless* we stipulate in addition that all have identical factor endowments.

Professor Samuelson has recently shown that if incomes were always optimally adjusted according to a consistent "welfare function," a community would provide us with a regular community indifference field with all the required properties.[15] This construction would yield both welfare inferences and demand relations. Each consistent welfare function will, however, generally yield a different community indifference map. Is there only one "true" welfare function which only the frailty of the human mind cannot always properly discern, or are there as many equally valid welfare functions as there are minds in the universe? The former view lies at the core of every totalitarian ideology; doubts as to its validity may be considered to be the essence of liberal skepticism.

The adjective "potential" in all the welfare criteria we have discussed emphasizes the *feasibility* of an improvement for every member of the community without necessarily indicating the *desirability* of the change, as has been stressed above. The case for or against a movement to the potentially better position is not prejudged. Unless accompanied by some scheme of redistributing income and wealth, a change leading to a higher welfare potential may conceivably be detrimental to the community at large, according to certain welfare judgments. Although this is largely a question of temperament, I would nevertheless hold that the burden of proof should always lie with the opponents of a "potential" improvement. Virtually none of the advances in technology and social organization that have lifted the human race to its present level of achievement have occurred without doing harm to somebody. If the extreme caution advocated by Little[16] *et al.* had always been practiced, we might not yet have made significant advances beyond the stone age—if we had ever gotten that far.

[15] "Social Indifference Curves," *Quarterly Journal of Economics*, **70** (1956), 1–22.

[16] I. M. D. Little, *A Critique of Welfare Economics* (2d ed.; Oxford: Clarendon Press, 1957).

# Bibliography

[This bibliography lists all books and articles cited in this monograph. It does not pretend to be a bibliography of the literature on flexible exchange rates.]

ADLER, J. H.; SCHLESINGER, E. R.; and WESTERBORG, E. VAN. *The Pattern of United States Import Trade since 1923.* New York: Federal Reserve Bank of New York, 1952.

ALEXANDER, S. S. "Devaluation versus Import Restriction as an Instrument for Improving Foreign Balance," *International Monetary Fund Staff Papers,* 1 (1950–51), 379–96.

———. "Effects of a Devaluation on a Trade Balance," *International Monetary Fund Staff Papers,* Vol. 2 (1951–52).

———. "Effects of a Devaluation: A Simplified Synthesis of Elasticities and Absorption Approaches," *American Economic Review,* 49 (1959), 22–42.

ALLEN, R. G. D. *Mathematical Analysis for Economists.* London: Macmillan, 1938.

ANGELL, J. W. "Equilibrium in International Trade: The United States 1919–26," *Quarterly Journal of Economics,* 42 (1928), 388–433.

ARROW, K. J., and DEBREU, G. "Existence of an Equilibrium for a Competitive Economy," *Econometrica,* 22 (1954), 289–90.

AUSPITZ, R. and LIEBEN, R. *Untersuchungen über die Theorie des Preises.* Leipzig: Duncker & Humblot, 1889.

BALDWIN, R. E. "Equilibrium in International Trade: A Diagrammatic Analysis," *Quarterly Journal of Economics,* 62 (1948), 748–62.

———. "The New Welfare Economics and Gains in International Trade," *Quarterly Journal of Economics,* 66 (1952), 91–101.

BALOGH, T., and STREETEN, P. P. "The Inappropriateness of Simple 'Elasticity' Concepts in the Analysis of International Trade," *Bulletin of the Oxford University Institute of Statistics,* 13 (1951), 65–77.

BANK OF CANADA. *Annual Report,* 1956.

BAUMOL, W. J. "Speculation, Profitability and Stability," *Review of Economics and Statistics,* 39 (1957), 263–71.

BENHAM, F. C. "The Terms of Trade," *Economica,* N.S., 7 (1940), 360–76.

BERNSTEIN, E. M. "Strategic Factors in Balance of Payments Adjustment," *International Monetary Fund Staff Papers,* 5 (1956), 151–69.

[ 157 ]

BHAGWATI, J. and JOHNSON, H. G. "Notes on Some Controversies in the Theory of International Trade," *Economic Journal*, 70 (1960), 74–93.

BLAU, G. "Some Aspects of the Theory of Futures Trading," *Review of Economic Studies*, 12 (1944–45), 1–30.

BLOOMFIELD, A. I. *Capital Imports and the American Balance of Payments 1934–39*. Chicago: University of Chicago Press, 1950.

BREMS, H. "Foreign Exchange Rates and Monopolistic Competition," *Economic Journal*, 63 (1953), 289–94.

BROWN, A. J. "Trade Balance and Exchange Stability," *Oxford Economic Papers*, Vol. 6 (1942).

CHANG, T. C. *Cyclical Movements in the Balance of Payments*. Cambridge: Cambridge University Press, 1951.

CHENG, H. S. "Statistical Estimates of Elasticities and Propensities in International Trade: A Survey of Published Studies," *International Monetary Fund Staff Papers*, 7 (1959), 107–58.

EASTMAN, H. C. "Aspects of Speculation in the Canadian Market for Foreign Exchange," *Canadian Journal of Economics and Political Science*, 24 (1958), 355–72.

EASTMAN, H. C., and STYKOLT, S. "Exchange Stabilization in Canada 1950–54," *Canadian Journal of Economics and Political Science*, 22 (1956), 221–33.

———. "Exchange Stabilization Further Considered," *Canadian Journal of Economics and Political Science*, 23 (1957), 404–8, with "Comment" by C. P. KINDLEBERGER.

EDGEWORTH, F. Y. "The Theory of International Values, I, II, III," *Economic Journal*, Vol. 4 (1894). Reprinted in F. Y. EDGEWORTH, *Papers Relating to Political Economy*, Vol. 2. London, 1925.

EINZIG, P. *The Theory of Forward Exchange*. London: Macmillan, 1937.

ELLSWORTH, P. T. "Exchange Rates and Exchange Stability," *Review of Economics and Statistics*, 32 (1950), 1–12.

FANNO, M. *Normal and Abnormal International Capital Transfers*. Minneapolis: University of Minnesota Press, 1939.

FLEMING, J. M. "On Making the Best of Balance of Payments Restrictions on Imports," *Economic Journal*, 61 (1951), 48–71.

———. "Exchange Depreciation, Financial Policy and the Domestic Price Level," *International Monetary Fund Staff Papers*, 6 (1958), 289–322.

FORD, A. G. "Flexible Exchange Rates and Argentina, 1885–1900," *Oxford Economic Papers*, N.S., Vol. 10 (1958).

FRIEDMAN, M. "The Case for Flexible Exchange Rates." In *Essays in Positive Economics*, pp. 157–203. Chicago: University of Chicago Press, 1953.

GRAAFF, J. DE V. "On Optimum Tariff Structures," *The Review of Economic Studies*, 17 (1949–50), 47–59.

[ 158 ]

GRADEN, V. "Effects of Multiple Exchange Rates," *Weltwirtschaftliches Archiv*, **81** (1958), 176–216.

GRAHAM, F. D. "International Trade under Depreciated Paper. The United States, 1862–1879," *Quarterly Journal of Economics*, **36** (1922), 227–73.

———. *The Cause and Cure of "Dollar Shortage."* ("Essays in International Finance," No. 10.) Princeton: Princeton University Press, 1949.

HABERLER, G. *The Theory of International Trade*. London: Hodge & Co., 1936.

———. *Prosperity and Depression*. 4th ed. Cambridge, Mass.: Harvard University Press, 1958.

———. "The Market of Foreign Exchange and Stability of the Balance of Payments," *Kyklos*, **3** (1949), 193–218.

———. "Currency Depreciation and the Terms of Trade." In *Wirtschaftliche Entwicklung und soziale Ordnung*, ed. E. LAGLER and J. MESSNER. Vienna: Herold, 1952.

———. *Currency Convertibility*. Washington: American Enterprise Association, 1954.

HAHN, L. A. *Geld und Kredit*. Frankfurt: Knapp, 1960.

HANSEN, B. "Interest Policy and Foreign Exchange Policy," *Skandinaviska Banken Quarterly Review*, October, 1958, pp. 114–22.

———. "Interest Policy, Foreign Exchange Policy and Foreign Exchange Control," *Skandinaviska Banken Quarterly Review*, January, 1959, pp. 15–28.

HARBERGER, A. C. "Currency Depreciation, Income and the Balance of Trade," *Journal of Political Economy*, **58** (1950), 47–60.

HARROD, R. F. "Convertibility Problems," *Economia Internazionale*, **8** (1955), 20–38.

———. *The Pound Sterling, 1951–1958*. ("Essays in International Finance," No. 30.) Princeton: Princeton University Press, 1958.

HAWTREY, R. G. *The Art of Central Banking*. London, 1932.

HENDERSON, SIR H. "The Function of Exchange Rates," *Oxford Economic Papers*, N.S., **1** (1949), 1–17.

HICKS, J. R. *Value and Capital*. 2d ed. London: Oxford University Press, 1946.

———. "The Valuation of the Social Income," *Economica*, N.S., **7** (1940), 105–24.

HINSHAW, R. "Currency Appreciation as an Anti-Inflationary Device," *Quarterly Journal of Economics*, Vol. **65** (1951).

HIRSCHMAN, A. O. "Devaluation and the Trade Balance," *Review of Economics and Statistics*, **31** (1949), 50–53.

HOUTHAKKER, H. S. "Can Speculators Forecast Prices?" *Review of Economics and Statistics*, **39** (1957), 143–51.

INTERNATIONAL MONETARY FUND. *Articles of Agreement.*

——. *Annual Report*, 1951.

——. *International Reserves and Liquidity.* Washington, 1958.

——. "The Adequacy of Monetary Reserves," *International Monetary Fund Staff Papers*, **3** (1953), 181–227.

IVERSEN, C. *Some Aspects of the Theory of International Capital Movements.* Copenhagen: Munksgaard, 1935.

JASAY, A. E. "Making Currency Reserves 'Go Round,'" *Journal of Political Economy*, **66** (1958), 353–56.

JOHNSON, H. G. *International Trade and Economic Growth.* Cambridge, Mass.: Harvard University Press, 1958.

——. "The Taxonomic Approach to Economic Policy," *Economic Journal*, **61** (1951), 812–32. "Addendum," *Economic Journal*, **63** (1953), 724–25.

KALDOR, N. "Speculation and Economic Stability," *Review of Economic Studies*, **7** (1939), 1–27.

KATZ, S. I. "Leads and Lags in Sterling Payments," *Review of Economics and Statistics*, **35** (1953), 75–80.

KEMP, M. C. "Unilateral Transfers and the Terms of Trade," *American Economic Review*, **46** (1956), 106–27.

KENEN, P. B. "On the Geometry of Welfare Economics," *Quarterly Journal of Economics*, **71** (1957), 426–47.

KEYNES, J. M. *Monetary Reform.* New York: Harcourt, Brace, 1924.

——. *A Treatise on Money.* New York: Harcourt, Brace, 1930.

——. *The General Theory of Employment, Interest and Money.* New York: Harcourt, Brace, 1936.

——. "The German Transfer Problem," *Economic Journal*, **39** (1929), 1–7. Reprinted in *Readings in the Theory of International Trade*, pp. 161–69.

——. "The Economic Consequences of Mr. Churchill." In *Essays in Persuasion*, pp. 244–70. London: Hart-Davis, 1931.

——. "The Future of the Foreign Exchanges," *Lloyds Bank Monthly Review*, October, 1935, pp. 527–35.

——. "Proposals for an International Clearing Union." London: H.M. Stationery Office, Cmd. 6437, April 7, 1943. Reprinted in *Federal Reserve Bulletin*, Vol. **29**, No. 6 (1943).

KINDLEBERGER, C. P. *International Short-Term Capital Movements.* New York: Columbia University Press, 1937.

——. "Speculation and Forward Exchange," *Journal of Political Economy*, **47** (1939), 163–81.

KLEIN, L. R. "The Empirical Foundations of Keynesian Economics." In *Post-Keynesian Economics*, ed. K. K. KURIHARA, pp. 277–319. New Brunswick, N.J.: Rutgers University Press, 1955.

LAURSEN, S., and METZLER, L. A. "Flexible Exchange Rates and the

Theory of Employment," *Review of Economics and Statistics*, 32 (1950), 281–99.

LEAGUE OF NATIONS (RAGNAR NURKSE). *International Currency Experience.* New York: Columbia University Press, 1944.

LERNER, A. P. "The Diagrammatical Representation of Cost Conditions in International Trade," *Economica*, 12 (1932), 346–56. Reprinted in A. P. LERNER, *Essays in Economic Analysis*, pp. 85–100. London: Macmillan, 1953.

———. *The Economics of Control.* New York: Macmillan, 1944.

LETICHE, J. M. *Balance of Payments and Economic Growth.* New York: Harper, 1959.

LIPSEY, R. G. and LANCASTER, R. K. "The General Theory of Second Best," *Review of Economic Studies*, 24 (1956–57), 11–32.

LITTLE, I. M. D. *A Critique of Welfare Economics.* 2d ed. Oxford: Clarendon Press, 1957.

LUTZ, F. A. "The Case for Flexible Exchange Rates," *Banca Nazionale del Lavoro Quarterly Review*, No. 31 (December, 1954), pp. 175–85.

MACDOUGALL, SIR DONALD. *The World Dollar Problem.* London: Macmillan, 1957.

———. "Flexible Exchange Rates," *Westminster Bank Review*, August, 1954.

MACHLUP, F. "The Theory of Foreign Exchanges," *Economica*, N.S., Vol. 6 (1939–40). Reprinted in *Readings in the Theory of International Trade*, pp. 104–58.

———. *International Trade and the National Income Multiplier.* Philadelphia: Blakiston, 1943.

———. "Elasticity Pessimism in International Trade," *Economia Internazionale*, 3 (1950), 118–37.

———. "Relative Prices and Aggregate Spending in the Analysis of Devaluation," *American Economic Review*, 45 (1955), 255–78.

———. "The Terms-of-Trade Effects of Devaluation upon Real Income and the Balance of Trade," *Kyklos*, Vol. 9 (1956).

MARSHALL, A. *The Pure Theory of Foreign Trade.* London, 1879. Reprinted in the series "Reprints of Scarce Tracts in Economic and Political Science," No. 1. London: London School of Economics and Political Science, 1930.

———. *Money, Credit and Commerce.* New York: Macmillan, 1924.

MEADE, J. E. *The Theory of International Economic Policy.* Vol. 1, *The Balance of Payments* and *Mathematical Supplement*. London: Oxford University Press, 1951; Vol. 2, *Trade and Welfare* and *Mathematical Supplement*. London: Oxford University Press, 1955.

———. *A Geometry of International Trade.* London: Allen & Unwin, 1952.

———. "The Case for Variable Exchange Rates," *Three Banks Review*, September, 1955.

MENDÈS-FRANCE, P. *Le redressement financier français en 1926 et 1927.* Paris: Librairie générale de droit et de jurisprudence, 1928.

METZLER, L. A. "The Transfer Problem Reconsidered," *Journal of Political Economy,* 50 (1942), 397–414. Reprinted in *Readings in the Theory of International Trade,* pp. 179–97.

————. "Tariffs, the Terms of Trade and the Distribution of the National Income," *Journal of Political Economy,* 57 (1949), 1–29.

————. "The Theory of International Trade." In *A Survey of Contemporary Economics,* ed. H. S. Ellis, 1, 210–54. Philadelphia: Blakiston, 1949).

MILL, J. S. *Principles of Political Economy.* Ed. SIR W. S. ASHLEY (1909). Reprinted by Longmans, Green & Co., London, 1936.

MINTS, L. *Monetary Policy for a Competitive Society.* New York: Macmillan, 1950.

MORGAN, D. J. and CORTLETT, W. J. "The Influence of Price in International Trade: A Study in Method," *Journal of the Royal Statistical Society,* Ser. A, Part III (1951), pp. 307–52.

MORGAN, E. V. "The Theory of Flexible Exchange Rates," *American Economic Review,* 45 (1955), 279–95.

MYRDAL, G. *An International Economy.* New York: Harper, 1956.

NURKSE, R. *Internationale Kapitalbewegungen.* Vienna: Springer, 1935.

————. *Conditions of International Monetary Equilibrium.* ("Essays in International Finance," No. 4.) Princeton: Princeton University Press, 1945. Reprinted in *Readings in the Theory of International Trade,* pp. 3–34.

OHLIN, B. *Interregional and International Trade.* Cambridge, Mass.: Harvard University Press, 1933.

————. "The Reparation Problem: A Discussion," *Economic Journal,* 39 (1929), 172–73. Reprinted in *Readings in the Theory of International Trade,* pp. 170–78.

ORCUTT, G. H. "Measurement of Price Elasticities in International Trade," *Review of Economics and Statistics,* 32 (1950), 117–32.

PEARCE, I. F. "A Note on Mr. Spraos' Paper," *Economica,* N.S., 22 (1955), 147–51.

POLAK, J. J., and CHANG, T. C. "Effect of Exchange Depreciation on a Country's Export Price Level," *International Monetary Fund Staff Papers,* 1 (1950–51), 49–70.

POLAK, J. J., and TA-CHUNG LIU, "Stability of the Exchange Rate Mechanism in a Multi-Country System," *Econometrica,* 22 (1954), 360–89.

*Readings in the Theory of International Trade.* American Economic Association. H. S. ELLIS and L. A. METZLER, eds. Philadelphia: Blakiston, 1950.

RHOMBERG, R. R. "Fluctuating Exchange Rates in Canada: Short-Term Capital Movements and Domestic Stability." Unpublished Ph.D. dissertation, Yale University, 1959.

———. "Canada's Foreign Exchange Market," *International Monetary Fund Staff Papers*, **7** (1960), 439–56.

ROBBINS, L. *The Economist in the Twentieth Century*. London: Macmillan, 1954.

ROBINSON, J. "The Foreign Exchanges." In *Essays in the Theory of Employment*. 2d ed. Oxford: Basil Blackwell, 1947. Reprinted in *Readings in the Theory of International Trade*, pp. 83–103.

———. "Beggar-My-Neighbour Remedies for Unemployment." In *Essays in the Theory of Employment*. 2d ed. Oxford: Blackwell, 1947. Reprinted in *Readings in the Theory of International Trade*, pp. 393–407.

SAMUELSON, P. A. *Foundations of Economic Analysis*. Cambridge, Mass.: Harvard University Press, 1947.

———. "Disparity in Postwar Exchange Rates." In *Foreign Economic Policy for the United States*, ed. S. E. HARRIS. Cambridge, Mass.: Harvard University Press, 1948.

———. "Evaluation of Real National Income," *Oxford Economic Papers*, N.S., **2** (1950), 1–29.

———. "The Transfer Problem and Transport Costs. Part I, The Terms of Trade When Impediments Are Absent," *Economic Journal*, **62** (1952), 278–304; Part II, "Analysis of Effects of Trade Impediments," *Economic Journal*, **64** (1954), 264–89.

———. "Social Indifference Curves," *Quarterly Journal of Economics*, **70** (1956), 1–22.

———. "Intertemporal Price Equilibrium: A Prologue to the Theory of Speculation," *Weltwirtschaftliches Archiv*, **79** (1957), 181–219.

SCAMMELL, W. M. *International Monetary Policy*. London: Macmillan, 1957.

———. "What Sort of Exchange Rates?" *Westminster Bank Review*, May, 1954.

SCHLESINGER, E. R. *Multiple Exchange Rates and Economic Development*. ("Princeton Studies in International Finance," No. 2.) Princeton: Princeton University Press, 1952.

SCITOVZKY, T. DE. "A Reconsideration of the Theory of Tariffs," *Review of Economic Studies*, **9** (1942), 89–110. Reprinted in *Readings in the Theory of International Trade*, pp. 358–89.

———. *Economic Theory and Western European Integration*. Stanford: Stanford University Press, 1958.

SHINOHARA, M. "The Multiplier and the Marginal Propensity To Import," *American Economic Review*, **47** (1957), 608–24.

[ 163 ]

SILVERMAN, A. G. "Some International Trade Factors for Great Britain," *Review of Economic Statistics*, **13** (1931), 114–24.

SOHMEN, E. "Demand Elasticities and the Foreign-Exchange Market," *Journal of Political Economy*, **65** (1957), 431–36.

———. "The Effect of Devaluation on the Price Level," *Quarterly Journal of Economics*, **72** (1958), 273–83, with "Comments" by J. VANEK and R. HINSHAW, pp. 614–32.

SPRAOS, J. "The Theory of Forward Exchange and Recent Practice," *The Manchester School*, **21** (1953), 87–117.

———. "Consumers' Behaviour and the Conditions for Exchange Stability," *Economica*, N.S., **22** (1955), 137–47.

———. "Stability in a Closed Economy and in the Foreign-Exchange Market, and the Redistributive Effect of Price Changes," *Review of Economic Studies*, **24** (1956–57), 161–76.

———. "Speculation, Arbitrage and Sterling," *Economic Journal*, **69** (1959), 1–21.

STACKELBERG, H. VON. "Die Theorie des Wechselkurses bei vollständiger Konkurrenz," *Jahrbücher für Nationalökonomie und Statistik*, **161** (1949), 1–65. Translated in "International Economic Papers," No. 1, pp. 104–59. London and New York: Macmillan, 1951.

STOLPER, W. F. and SAMUELSON, P. A. "Protection and Real Wages," *Review of Economic Studies*, **9** (1941), 58–73. Reprinted in *Readings in the Theory of International Trade*, pp. 333–57.

———. "The Multiplier, Flexible Exchanges, and International Equilibrium," *Quarterly Journal of Economics*, **64** (1950), 59–82.

STUVEL, G. *The Exchange Stability Problem*. New York: Kelley, 1951.

TAUSSIG, F. W. *International Trade*. New York: Macmillan, 1927.

———. "International Trade under Depreciated Paper," *Quarterly Journal of Economics*, **31** (1917), 380–403. "Comment" by J. H. HOLLANDER and "Rejoinder," *Quarterly Journal of Economics*, **32** (1918), 674–94.

TELSER, L. G. "A Theory of Speculation Relating Profitability and Stability," with "Reply" by W. J. BAUMOL, *Review of Economics and Statistics*, **41** (1959), 295–302.

TRIFFIN, R. *Europe and the Money Muddle*. New Haven: Yale University Press, 1957.

———. "The Return to Convertibility: 1926–1931 and 1958——?" *Banca Nazionale del Lavoro Quarterly Review*, No. 48 (1959), pp. 3–57. Reprinted in *Gold and the Dollar Crisis*. New Haven: Yale University Press, 1960.

———. "Tomorrow's Convertibility: Aims and Means of International Monetary Policy," *Banca Nazionale del Lavoro Quarterly Review*, No. 49 (1959), pp. 131–200. Reprinted in *Gold and the Dollar Crisis*. New Haven: Yale University Press, 1960.

TSIANG, S. C. "An Experiment with a Flexible Exchange Rate System: The Case of Peru, 1950–54," *International Monetary Fund Staff Papers*, **5** (1957), 449–76.

———. "A Theory of Foreign-Exchange Speculation under a Floating Exchange System," *Journal of Political Economy*, **66** (1958), 399–418.

———. "The Theory of Forward Exchange and Effects of Government Intervention on the Forward Exchange Market," *International Monetary Fund Staff Papers*, **7** (1959), 75–106.

———. "Fluctuating Exchange Rates in Countries with Relatively Stable Economies: Some European Experiences after World War I," *International Monetary Fund Staff Papers*, **7** (1959), 244–73.

U TUN WAI. "The Relation between Inflation and Economic Development: A Statistical Inductive Study," *International Monetary Fund Staff Papers*, **7** (1959), 302–17.

UNITED NATIONS. *The International Flow of Private Capital, 1946–1952.* New York, 1954.

———. *The International Flow of Private Capital, 1956–1958.* New York, 1959.

VINER, J. *Canada's Balance of International Indebtedness 1900–1913.* Cambridge, Mass.: Harvard University Press, 1924.

———. *Studies in the Theory of International Trade.* New York: Harper, 1937.

———. "Some International Aspects of Economic Stabilization." In L. D. WHITE (ed.), *The State of the Social Sciences*, pp. 283–98. Chicago: Chicago University Press, 1956.

WHITE, H. D. *The French International Accounts 1880–1913.* Cambridge, Mass.: Harvard University Press, 1933.

WHITE, W. H. "The Employment-Insulating Advantages of Flexible Exchanges: A Comment on Professors Laursen and Metzler," *Review of Economics and Statistics*, **36** (1954), 225–28.

WILLIAMS, J. H. *Argentine International Trade under Inconvertible Paper Money: 1880–1900.* Cambridge, Mass.: Harvard University Press, 1920.

# Index

Absorption: defined, 30; and balance on current account, 33 ff., 106 ff.; distinguished from income effects, 39–40

Adjustable peg: and trade restrictions, 33, 114; and exchange risks, 119, 132; and international lending, 120, 131–33; and inflation, 128; and speculation, 130

Adler, J. H., 16 n., 157

Alexander, S. S., 5 n., 14–15, 30 n., 33 n., 35 n., 41, 42, 91 n., 148 n., 157

Allen, R. G. D., 48 n., 68 n., 94 n., 157

Allocation of resources: and balance on current account, 33, 41 n., 110 n.; and trade restrictions, 104; and index-number criteria, 107; and adjustable peg, 114; and multiple-exchange rates, 121; and inflation, 127–28; under autarky, 142

Angell, J. W., 37 n., 157

Arbitrage and exchange-market stability, 13, 23, 75. *See also* Interest arbitrage

Arrow, K. J., 11–12, 157

Auspitz, R., 148 n., 157

Autarky, welfare aspects, 142–46

Baldwin, R. E., 141 n., 149 n., 157

Balogh, T., 6 n., 157

Bank of Canada, 130, 157

Bank deposits and movements of gold and capital, 20 ff., 61

Bank rate (Canada), floating, 130

Bank-rate policy and capital movements: under flexible exchange rates, 72–76, 80–90; under the gold standard, 72, 76, 78

Baumol, W. J., 45 n., 48 n., 55, 56, 157

Benham, F. C., 32 n., 157

Bernstein, E. M., 103 n., 157

Bhagwati, J., 9–11, 158

Bilateral monopoly of stabilization funds, 12

Blau, G., 65 n., 158

Bloomfield, A. I., 19 n., 158

Boulding, K. E., 139

Brems, H., 16 n., 158

Brown, A. J., 5 n., 6 n., 158

Calculus of variations, 49

Capital account of the balance of payments, 18, 92 n., 129

Capital flight: and inflation, 28, 88, 134; and terms of trade, 122; and pegged exchange rates, 133

Capital movements: freedom of, 13, 25, 69, 120, 123, 138; and foreign-exchange market, 19; predictability under flexible exchanges, 19; monetary effects under pegged and under flexible exchange rates, 22, 28–29; income effects of, 25–29, 38, 100; long-term, 26–27, 101, 130 ff.; short-term, 27 ff.; and bank-rate policy, 72–76, 83–90; under flexible exchanges (Canada and Argentina), 132. *See also* Interest arbitrage; Speculation

Central bank intervention: on forward exchange markets, 12 n., 60, 83–84, 87–90, 100, 136–38; on exchange markets, 21 ff.

Chang, T. C., 16 n., 32 n., 158, 162

Cheng, H. S., 16 n., 158

Churchill, W. S., 125 n.

Commodities, "international" and "domestic," 40

Commodity arbitrage and exchange-market stability, 13, 23, 75

[ 167 ]

Community indifference curves, 145, 154; Scitovsky type, 151; Samuelson type, 155

Comparative advantage: and balance on current account, 33; and terms of trade, 34, 41; and index-number criteria, 107; and discrimination against luxuries, 109 n.; and inflation, 134; geometric demonstration, 144–45

Compensatory official financing, defined, 18

Consumption function, 93–94

Controls. *See* Exchange controls; Trade restrictions

Cortlett, W. J., 17 n., 162

Cost-inflation: and balance on current account, 39; and depreciation, 127

Countercyclical policy, and flexible exchange rates, 24, 29, 43, 83–90, 100 n., 115, 123–24, 135

Credit rationing and allocation of resources, 128

Creeping inflation, 127–28

Cross-elasticities of demand, 2, 26

Current account of the balance of payments, 1 ff.; and depreciation, 5 ff., 32 ff., 104; measurement in domestic and in foreign currency, 9 n.; and terms of trade, 41; and monetary policy, 83 ff.

Debreu, G., 11–12, 157

Deflation: and capital movements, 26–27; and trade liberalization, 108; as a cure for overvaluation, 125, 131; in the United Kingdom, Germany, the United States, 125

Demand for foreign exchange, derivation, 3

Depreciation and devaluation: and balance on current account, 5 ff., 32 ff., 103–6; and inflation, 7 n., 102 ff., 125–27; and terms of trade, 34; under conditions of underemployment, 104

Devaluation: of Austrian schilling (1953), 111; of pound sterling (1949), 111, 119

Discommodities, 11

Discount rate. *See* Bank rate

Discrimination by soft-currency countries, 108

Domestic commodities, 40

Duesenberry, J., 94 n.

Eastman, H. C., 59 n., 136 n., 158

Economic development. *See* Underdeveloped areas

Edgeworth, F. Y., 148 n., 158

Edgeworth-Bowley box, 150–51

Einzig, P., 50 n., 65 n., 71, 76 n., 81 n., 137, 138 n., 158

Elasticities: and exchange-market stability, 4 ff.; short-run, 13, 23; of demand, measurement, 16; and terms of trade, 32

Elasticities of forward exchange market schedules, 73–74; and speculation, 80 ff.; and central bank intervention, 87–90

Elasticity approach, 1 n.

Elasticity of expectations, 52 ff.

Elasticity, partial, 2

Elasticity, total, 2, 5, 44, 96 n.

Elasticity pessimism, 5 ff.; and fluctuating exchange rates, 11 ff.; and appreciation of D-Mark, 15; and infant-industry argument for protection, 15

Elasticity of supply of funds for interest arbitrage, 70–71, 74 n., 77

Ellis, H. S., 61 n., 162

Ellsworth, P. T., 6 n., 158

Equilibrium in foreign-exchange markets, 4 ff., 52, 103; welfare aspects of, 116–18

Exchange controls: and exchange-rate stability, 24; and balance on current account, 33, 103; welfare aspects of, 34, 103–7, 114–17; and forward discount, 69; and pegged exchange rates, 79, 134; inflationary effect of, 108–9; and capital movements, 133–34

Exchange rates: defined, 3 n.; negative, 9

Exchange risks: and forward exchange market, 65 ff., 88, 137; and adjustable peg, 119–20, 131 ff.

Expectations, 46, 52 ff., 100; interaction of, 57; and forward markets, 80 ff.; and real rate of interest, 82

Exports and supply of foreign exchange, 3 ff.

Fanno, M., 19 n., 158

Fiscal policy: and foreign-exchange reserves, 14; and transfer, 31, 34; under gold standard or pegged exchange rates, 79, 114, 123

[ 168 ]

Fleming, J. M., 148 n., 158

Flexibility pessimism, 6

Flexible exchange rates: in France, 58; in the United Kingdom, 58, 121; in Canada, 59, 116, 124, 132, 138–39; in Lebanon, 59, 124, 139 n.; in Peru, 59; in Argentina, 116, 124, 132, 139 n.

Fluctuating exchange rates. *See* Flexible exchange rates

Ford, A. G., 132, 158

Foreign aid, 105, 130, 132

Foreign-exchange reserves: and balance of payments, 14, 18, 103, 105, 118, 134; of commercial banks, 22; and interest arbitrage, 89–90, 118, 137; and leads and lags, 118; and inflation, 126–28; and forward-market operations by central banks, 136–37

Foreign investment, 26–27, 87, 101, 130 ff.; and exchange controls, 131–33

Foreign-trade multiplier, 62–64

Foresight of speculators, 46 ff., 56 ff., 135; and forward markets, 75, 80 ff.; and gold standard, 76 ff.

Forward exchange market: and hedging, 65, 72–76; depth of forward exchange market and effectiveness of bank-rate policy, 74–75, 87–90; multiple forward markets with different maturities, 88–89; bankers' attitude toward forward markets, 137–38. *See also* Central bank intervention on forward exchange markets

Forward premium (or discount): and interest differential, 68; and speculation, 69

Free entry in speculative markets, 49, 51, 56

Free goods, 11

Free trade, potential superiority over autarky, 144–46

Friedman, M., 6 n., 45 n., 52 n., 54, 94 n., 119 n., 136, 158

Full employment: and capital movements, 27 ff.; and balance on current account, 33, 63, 128–29. *See also* Countercyclical policy

Fundamental disequilibrium, 112, 114

Futures markets, 65 n., 71

Gains from trade, 144 ff.

General equilibrium, 2, 11 n., 110

Giffen's paradox, 7, 95, 97, 153

Gold arbitrage, 61, 78

Gold-exchange standard, 129

Gold movements: monetary effects, 20, 60–61; importance for gold-standard adjustment, 22, 61–64, 72; and absorption, 36, 63–64

Gold points: and boundaries of exchange-rate fluctuation under a paper standard, 20, 25, 79; and gold flows, 36, 61–64, 77–78; and bank-rate policy, 77–78, 84; and fiscal policy, 79

Gold price, 137

Gold standard: and paper standard, real and imagined differences, 21, 77–79, 81–83; price and income effects, 35 ff.; and speculation, 60–64; and forward markets, 76 ff.

Government guarantees against exchange risks, 131

Graaff, J. de V., 141 n., 148 n., 158

Graden, V., 121 n., 159

Graham, F. D., 40, 119 n., 159

Haberler, G., 3, 6 n., 12 n., 23 n., 26 n., 30 n., 33 n., 119 n., 124 n., 159

Hahn, L. A., 159

Hansen, A. H., 70 n.

Hansen, B., 79 n., 159

Harberger, A. C., 5 n., 91 n., 159

Harris, S. E., 6 n.

Harrod, Sir Roy, 6 n., 102 n., 137 n., 159

Hawtrey, R. G., 69 n., 159

Hedging: and forward exchange markets, 65, 73, 88, 89, 120; against inflation, 127

Henderson, Sir Hubert, 159

Hicks, J. R., 52–53, 56, 147, 150 n., 151, 152, 159

Hinshaw, R., 102 n., 103 n., 159

Hirschman, A. O., 5 n., 9 n., 159

Homogeneous functions, 93–94

Houthakker, H. S., 159

Hume, D., 60

Idle cash balances: and interest arbitrage, 69; and monetary policy, 70

Import restrictions. *See* Exchange controls; Trade restrictions

Imports and demand for foreign exchange, 3 ff.

Income effects: and total elasticities, 2, 5; of speculative capital movements, 28; and balance-of-payments adjustment, 35–38, 61–64; distinguished from absorption, 39–40

Income redistribution and potential welfare, 106 n., 117, 146–55

Index-number criteria for changes in real income and price level, 106–11, 149–55

Index-number problems, 30 n., 36, 93 n.

Indifference maps, 142 ff. *See also* Community indifference maps

Inflation: and depreciation, 7 n., 102 ff., 125–27, 133; effect of capital movements, 27–29; and capital flight, 28, 88, 134; cost-inflation and balance on current account, 39; and foreign-exchange reserves, 89–90, 118; effect of trade restrictions, 103, 108–9; encouraged or inhibited by exchange-rate flexibility, 124–27; creeping, 127–28; and full employment, 128; and pegged exchange rates, 128, 132

Instability in foreign-exchange markets, 4 ff.

Interest arbitrage: defined, 64; analysis, 65 ff., 86; and gold points, 77–78; and Marshall-Lerner condition, 85; and foreign-exchange reserves, 89–90, 118, 137

Interest differential and forward premium (discount), 68, 72

Interest-elasticity of saving and investment, 35–39, 63–64

Interest rate, real: and balance on current account, 39; and monetary policy, 82–83

International Clearing Union (Keynes plan), 113 n.

International liquidity, 89–90, 129; and inflation, 128; and forward-market operations by central banks, 136–37

International Monetary Fund, 112–15, 119, 132 n., 137 n., 139 n., 160; proposed reforms, 129

International transmission of business cycles: under pegged exchange rates, 92; under flexible exchange rates, 92, 99, 100 n.

Interpersonal comparisons of utility, 141, 147 n., 148, 153

Inventories: and transfer mechanism, 27, 32; of speculators, 48, 57; and foreign-trade multiplier, 63; and futures markets, 71

Investment: interest-elasticity of, 35–39, 63–64; and inflation, 128

Iversen, C., 19 n., 160

Jasay, A. E., 90, 137, 160

Johnson, H. G., 9–11, 23 n., 30 n., 33, 42, 43 n., 91 n., 110 n., 158, 160

Kaldor, N., 48 n., 147, 152, 160

Kaldor-Hicks welfare criterion, 151, 52

Katz, S. I., 118 n., 160

Kemp, M. C., 43 n., 160

Kenen, P. B., 141 n., 148 n., 160

Keynes, J. M., 25, 40 n., 41 n., 42–44, 58, 60, 66, 69 n., 72, 73 n., 74, 76, 79, 80, 83, 89, 90, 113, 120, 123, 125 n., 138 n., 160

Kindleberger, C. P., 19 n., 72, 73 n., 76, 83, 136 n., 158, 160

Klein, L. R., 35 n., 160

Lancaster, R. K., 116 n., 161

Laspeyres' price index, 106–8, 111 n.

Laursen, S., 5 n., 6 n., 24 n., 91 n., 92, 93 n., 95 n., 96 n., 98–100, 160

Laursen-Metzler effect, 99–100

"Leads and lags" and foreign-exchange reserves, 118

Lerner, A. P., 5 n., 55, 139, 145 n., 161

Letiche, J. M., 44 n., 161

Lieben, R., 148 n., 157

Lipsey, R. G., 116 n., 161

Little, I. M. D., 147, 155, 161

Liu, Ta-Chung, 11 n., 162

Lutz, F. A., 55, 119 n., 161

Luxury goods: welfare effects of trade restrictions on, 109; and multiple-exchange rates, 121

MacDougall, Sir Donald, 119 n., 161

Machlup, F., 3, 12 n., 16 n., 21 n., 32 n., 33, 43, 61 n., 161

Macroeconomics: and the theory of international trade, 43–44, 61–64, 91, 110, 114; and underdeveloped areas, 132

Marginal productivity of capital and long-term capital movements, 26

Marginal propensity to consume and terms of trade, 41 n.

Marginal propensity to import, 30 n., 44, 62, 96 n.

Marginal rates of substitution: and inflation, 127; in consumption and production, 141

Marshall, A., 5, 9, 10, 161

Marshall-Lerner condition, 5, 8, 13, 85, 92; and terms-of-trade effect of devaluation, 12 n.

Maximum-likelihood estimation, analogy, 46

Meade, J. E., 6 n., 9, 18 n., 30 n., 31, 41 n., 45 n., 55, 117 n., 119 n., 136 n., 161

Mendès-France, P., 59 n., 162

Metzler, L. A., 5 n., 6 n., 15 n., 24 n., 42 n., 43, 61 n., 91 n., 92, 93 n., 95 n., 96 n., 98–100, 160, 162

Mill, J. S., 31 n., 36 n., 55, 162

Mint parities, 60

Mints, L., 162

Modigliani, F., 94 n.

Monetary effects: of capital movements, 20 ff., 126; two varieties distinguished, 27

Monetary policy: and foreign-exchange reserves, 14; and capital movements, 29, 72 ff., 83 ff.; and absorption, 34–35; and speculation, 54, 81–83; and idle cash balances, 70; and gold points (or exchange-rate pegs), 77–79, 114, 123 ff.; and expectations, 82–83; under flexible exchange rates, 83–90, 100, 115, 123–24

Monopoly and elasticity pessimism, 16

Montias, J. M., 139 n.

Morgan, D. J., 17 n., 162

Morgan, E. V., 6 n., 162

Multiple equilibria, 4, 8 ff., 116 n.

Multiple-exchange rates, 121–23; "multiflex" system, 122

Multiplier effects of foreign trade, 62–64

Myrdal, G., 105 n., 162

National-income analysis. See Macroeconomics

Nurkse, R., 19 n., 50 n., 52, 58, 103 n., 120 n., 138 n., 139 n., 161, 162

Offer curves, 10

Ohlin, B., 40, 41 n., 162

Oligopoly in speculative markets, 59

"Optimum" tariff, 148, 154; and exchange controls, 34, 108–9

Orcutt, G. H., 16 n., 162

Overvaluation, 102–3, 114–17, 120, 130 ff.; and capital movements, 105–6, 130 ff.; deflation as a cure for, 125

Paasche's price index, 106–8, 111 n.

Par values, 112

Pareto optimum: and equilibrium in the foreign-exchange market, 116–18; in world production, 145

Partial-equilibrium demand curve, 2

Pearce, I. F., 91 n., 162

Pegged exchange rates, pure case, 21

Polak, J. J., 11 n., 32 n., 162

Potential welfare: and depreciation, 13–14; and index-number criteria, 106; and trade controls, 107, 148; and new commodities, 108; defined, 145

Price controls and effects of depreciation, 110

Price discrimination through multiple-exchange rates, 121

Price effects under the gold standard, 35; inconsistencies in the classical version, 36–37, 61 n.

Price flexibility and fluctuating exchange rates, 26, 29, 84–85

Price-level changes: and balance-of-payments adjustment, 36–40, 60–62; sectional price levels, 36 n., 40; and aggregate demand, 92 ff.; and index numbers, 106–11; and profits of importers, 110

Price stability: and pegged exchange rates, 123; and economic growth, 127, 133; policy goal, 135

Principle of insufficient reason and "second-best" welfare economics, 117

Profit-maximization and stabilizing speculation, 45, 54 ff., 80 ff., 136

Protective subsidies to (instead of duties on) imports, 15

Purchasing power shifts and balance-of-payments adjustment, 39–40

Quantity theory of money, 61

Quotas. See Trade restrictions

PRINTED IN U.S.A.